Pin Loom Weaving

Pin Loom Weaving

40 Projects for Tiny Hand Looms

MARGARET STUMP

STACKPOLE
BOOKS

Published by
STACKPOLE BOOKS
5067 Ritter Road
Mechanicsburg, PA 17055
www.stackpolebooks.com

Printed in the United States of America

First edition

Cover design by Tessa J. Sweigert

Cataloging-in-Publication Data is on file with the Library of Congress.

ISBN 978-0-8117-1248-4

Contents

Introduction

Welcome to the world of the pin loom! This book is for pin loom weavers and for people looking for a craft that is personal, portable, versatile, and fun. With a pin loom, you can weave a piece of cloth in minutes rather than hours or days. Pin looms allow you to easily indulge your need to create with fiber. They are simple enough for kids to use, but offer a depth of challenge to experienced fiber artists and crafters.

This book offers contemporary techniques and projects to use with old and new pin looms alike. First introduced in the 1930s, pin looms have been known by a variety of names including Weave-It, Loomette, and Jiffy Loom. Many of today's pin loom weavers were first introduced to weaving through a grandmother's Weave-It loom. The pin loom was commonly used until the early 1970s, when, due to a generational change and waning interest, they retreated to sewing boxes and attics.

Then something wonderful happened. Pin loom weavers and people who remembered pin loom weaving got together over the internet. Many old pin looms, still sturdy and looking good as new, became available for sale through eBay. In response to the renewed interest in the craft, new pin looms, like the Weavette and the Schacht Zoom Loom, appeared on the market. The only thing needed was contemporary ideas for projects to match the times. And that is what *Pin Loom Weaving* offers you.

If there is a problem with pin looms, it is that the weaving process is so darned addictive. (There. I've said it and I take no further responsibility for any problems experienced as a result of this craft, including but not limited to loss of sleep and yarn addiction.) My journey with weavies began with and has been sustained by the sense of delight I feel from weaving on the little looms. There is a sense of magic in being able to wind yarn onto a loom, weave it through, and finish with a unique piece of cloth that has a perfect selvedge edge all around.

The only drawback was that after getting drawn into this magic, I found myself with hundreds of weavies and asking "Now what do I do with all these damn squares?" I searched for project ideas, looking at the patterns originally written in the '30s and '40s. I noticed that the patterns shared a common strategy: They tried to assemble the squares in a way that would make the project look like it was created from whole cloth—and, in that, they failed miserably. They ignored a basic quality of the weavie—that it is a small and complete piece of cloth.

I wondered how I might take another path, find a way to *celebrate* the unique size and completeness of these woven squares rather than try to make them into something they were not. I found my best and happiest weaving path by looking to an exemplar of art and craft, the Amish quilt. In looking at those timeless and exquisite creations, I am reminded that things are often loveliest when they best and most simply express themselves. In each of my patterns, I have tried to create something that truly expresses the pin loom and its unique product, the weavie.

Whether you are looking for simple or complex projects, for a jumping-off place for your next creation or complete instructions to carry you through from start to finish, you will find it here. In addition to a wide variety of pin loom projects, I have included instructions for several popular approaches for joining the weavies and a selection of weaving patterns. I hope you have as much fun making these items as I have.

CHAPTER ONE

Tools and Skills

Looms and Other Tools

Looms

You can make the items in this book using any hand loom that is more or less the right size.

All of the projects were created on handheld looms based on the design of the Weave-It Loom, originally manufactured in the '30s, '40s, and '50s. Although the

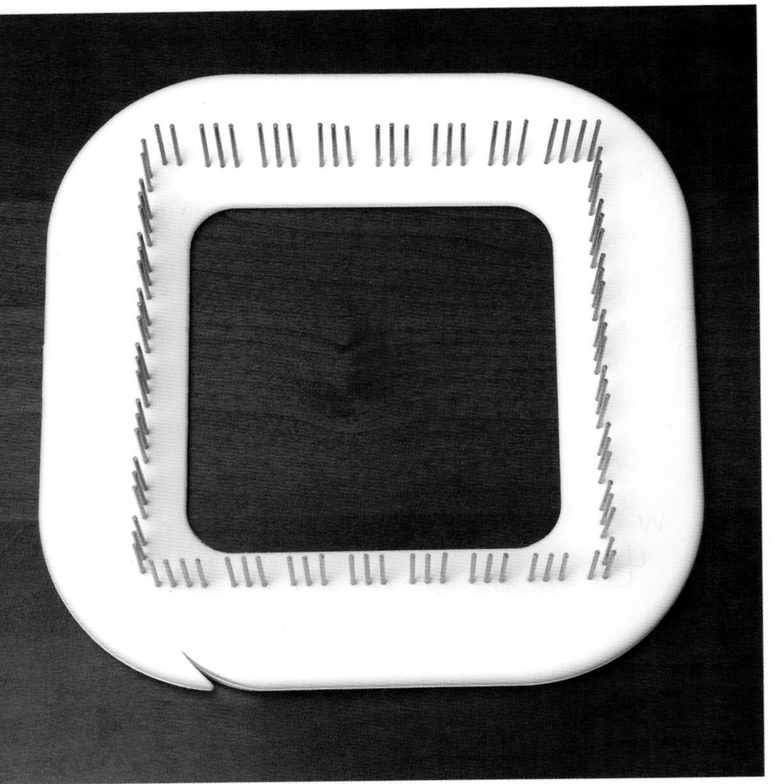

The Zoom Loom, a pin loom made and sold by the Schacht Spindle Company

Weave-It was the most popular, there were many different hand looms available (including Loomette and Jiffy Loom), and weavers are still happily using them today. You can often find old looms in good condition available through eBay or other auction sites.

You can also build a hand loom of your own in any size. Step-by-step instructions for building your own loom begin on page 4.

There are a growing number of craftsmen and businesses now producing beautiful hand looms. Check the resources on page 124 for a list of manufacturers, but consider checking online as well, since that list will likely grow and change over time.

Keep in mind that you don't have to have every loom that is called for. You can join squares or "weavies" (a term for the products of the little looms, which are often not square) in order to produce the dimensions called for in a specific pattern. For example, if the pattern calls for 2" x 4" weavies, you can make twice as many 2" x 2" weavies and join them together.

The following loom sizes are used to make the projects in this book:

- 2" x 2" (5 x 5 cm)
- 2" x 4" (5 x 10 cm)
- 4" x 4" (10 x 10 cm)
- 4" x 6" (10 x 15 cm)
- 6" x 6" (15 x 15 cm)

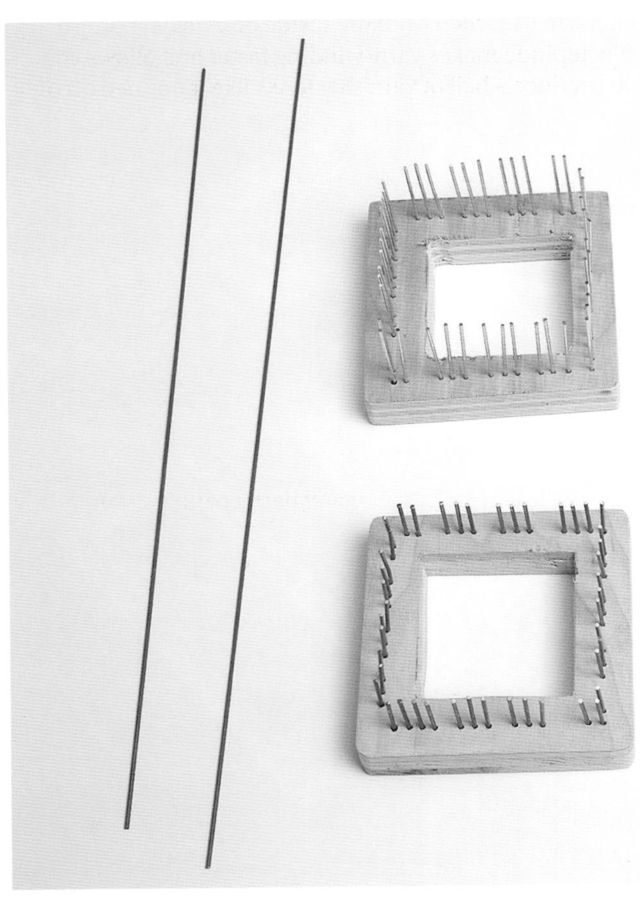

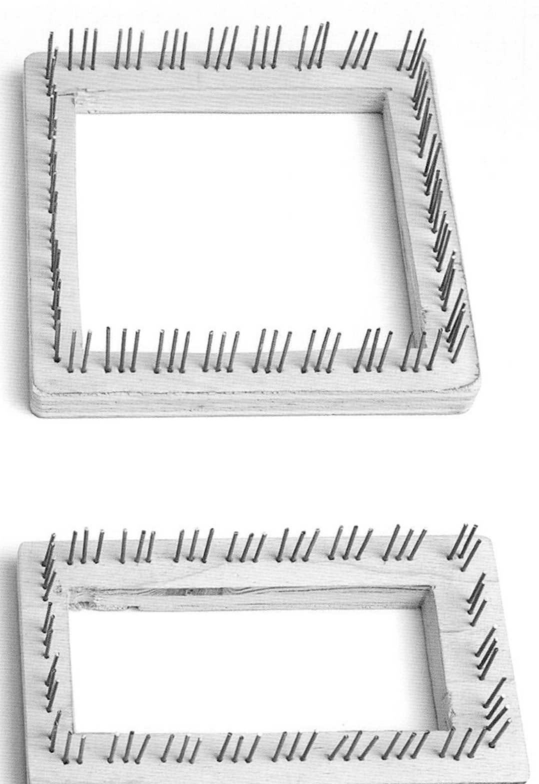

Homemade looms in various sizes

Essential Tools

Weaving needle. In addition to a pin loom, you need a needle that is thin enough to fit between the pins and long enough to span the width of the loom with enough needle left over to pull through. Optimally, that means that for a 2" loom you need a 4" needle, for a 4" loom, you need a 6" needle, and for a 6" loom you need an 8" needle.

The needle should have a rounded tip so that it doesn't split the yarn when you weave with it. If you cannot find a needle with a rounded tip, you can round off the tip of a pointed needle using a fine-cut flat file or a whetstone. In order to form a rounded tip, the needle needs to be moved in a smooth arc over the file rather than just rubbing it in one plane, which will produce a flat end. If you have a bench grinder with a stone, hold the needle against the moving stone, again keeping in mind that the needle needs to be moved in an arc-like fashion to produce the rounded tip. You can find suggestions of specific sources for suitable weaving needles in the resources section on page 124.

Crochet hook. Many of the projects use crochet edging and joining. All the crochet work is extremely simple, consisting mainly of single crochet. I primarily used a size G-6 (4.0 mm) hook for most of the projects. I also have a size F-5 (3.75 mm) hook that I use if I get into a tight space and the other one seems a little too big. You want to use a size that produces a chain that matches the size of the weavies' edge loops. The G hook accomplishes that for me, but you may find you are more comfortable with a hook that is a little bigger or a little smaller.

Tapestry needle. A tapestry needle is necessary for several joining methods and helpful for running yarn ends back into the woven cloth.

Optional Tools

Fork. This can be a really helpful tool during the weaving process. You can use the fork as a beater and separator after each row to straighten the weaving, press down the completed rows, and open up the next row so that it is easier to weave. Many pin loom weavers just use their needle to straighten and beat down the previous line of weaving, but I like the fork because it does a more complete job and because it keeps the essential weaving needle from being bowed or bent. My personal preference is to use an old-fashioned, long-tined fork both because the shape works very well and because it feels good to work with pretty tools. You can find old forks in many thrift or collectible shops.

Small crochet hook. In addition to the larger hook used for joining, a small crochet hook will be helpful for cleaning up any stray yarn ends. One of the last steps I take when I finish an item is to use the small crochet hook to catch the ends left over from joining and pull them back into the material. It looks better than just tying off and cutting the loose ends, and ensures that the knots do not come loose. I would suggest a very small regular crochet hook or a larger steel hook—something between 1.7 and 2.25 mm.

PVC Nøstepinde. The original Nøstepinde is a Swedish invention, a turned hardwood stick about 8" (20 cm) long that allows you to easily wind balls of yarn that can be pulled from the inside or outside. Using a Nøstepinde makes yarn-winding faster and allows you to produce a ball of yarn that looks like it popped off of a mechanical yarn winder.

I substitute a 9" to 12" piece of electrical PVC conduit for the traditional carved stick. PVC pipe is available at any hardware store, costs pennies per foot, and can usually be cut to whatever length you want. It is very light and comfortable to hold. And unlike with the solid stick, you can run your starting yarn end down the tube to get it out of the way while you wind the yarn ball. Sand the ends so that they don't snag the yarn, and follow any of the multitude of written or video directions available on the internet on how to wind the ball. It takes a little practice to get comfortable winding yarn this way, but the yarn balls you make are nearly perfect and will smoothly feed from the middle.

Making Your Own Loom

If you aren't able to find a convenient commercial source, or if you want a nonstandard size pin loom, you might want to make your own. It requires just a few materials and some basic skills for working with wood and wire. Follow the directions here, and you can have a handmade loom of your own in an afternoon or two (bigger sizes will require a little more time because they have more pins).

Before we start, let's talk for a minute about what to use for pins. The pins in the early pin looms are about 0.03" in diameter. Wire brads or other small nails aren't a good substitute because they are too thick and won't leave enough space for your weaving needle to pass between them (weaving needles typically measure 0.065" to 0.075" in diameter).

I've found two good possibilities for the pins: 0.039" music wire or #5 embroidery needles. Since these are actually about the same diameter as the original pins, they leave ample room for your weaving needle to fit between them. Both materials are stiff enough to be driven in with a small hammer. Music wire is available at many chain craft stores or can be ordered online. Embroidery needles are also available at craft stores as well as at general department stores and most sewing and fabric shops.

Some preparation of the pins is needed. Cut music wire into 1⅛" to 1¼" lengths with sturdy wire cutters; cut on a diagonal to produce a sharp end that will allow you to drive the wire into the frame. Use pliers to break off the eyes of the needles. For both materials, smooth the tops of the pins with a fine flat file to eliminate any rough edges that could snag or split the yarn before driving them in place.

Plywood is a better choice for making pin looms than a solid piece of wood. Solid wood blanks tend to split when you set the pins. For best results, use baltic birch plywood, available from premium woodworking supply retailers.

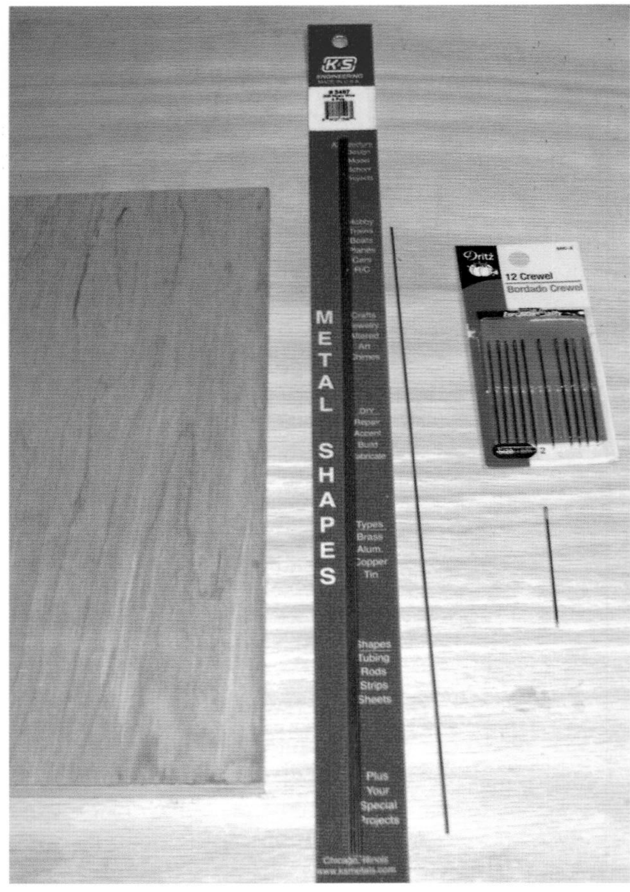

Materials

- A piece of ½" (1.25 cm) hardwood plywood, a little wider than the size of loom you want to make and several inches longer (to provide room to clamp it down)
- 0.039" (1 mm) music wire, about 1¼" for every pin needed (I recommend K & S Engineering's part number 5497, available online from craft, hobby, and home improvement stores), or #5 embroidery needles (one needle per pin)

Tools

- Scissors
- Single-edge razor blade or craft knife
- Handsaw or table saw
- Clamp
- Drill with ¼" or ⅜" bit
- Saber or coping saw
- Small hammer
- Pliers or flat-bladed screwdriver
- Diagonal wire cutters
- Sanding block and sandpaper
- Fine flat file or thread file

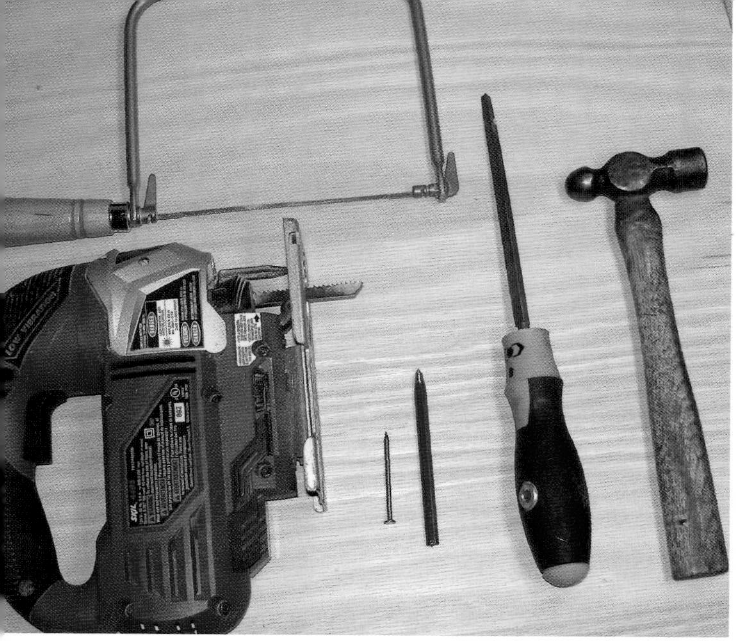

Instructions

1. Decide what size of loom you want to build. The templates in the book can be used as is or as a guide for making other dimensions.

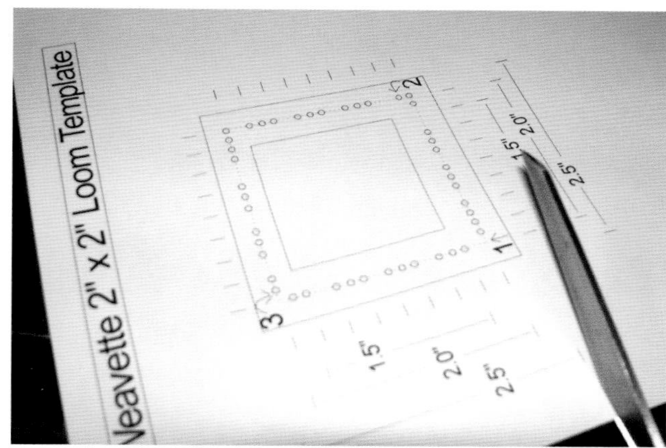

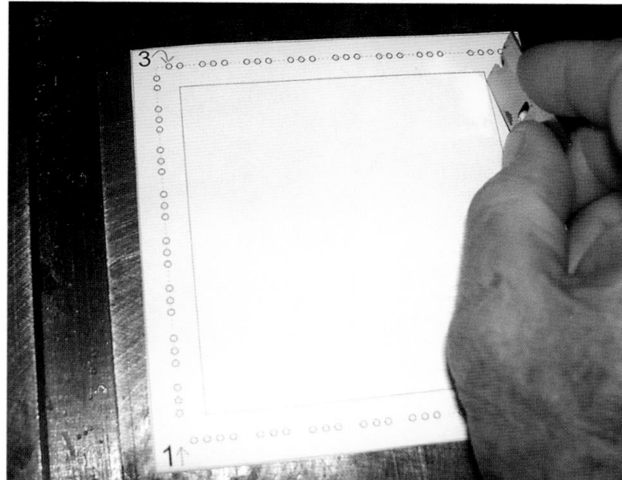

2. Photocopy the template page at the size you want and cut it out. Use a razor blade or X-acto knife to remove the inside portion.

3. Next, cut the plywood base to the right width. (Wait until step 7 to cut the piece to the correct length; this leaves you with some extra to use to clamp the base down while you saw out the center.)

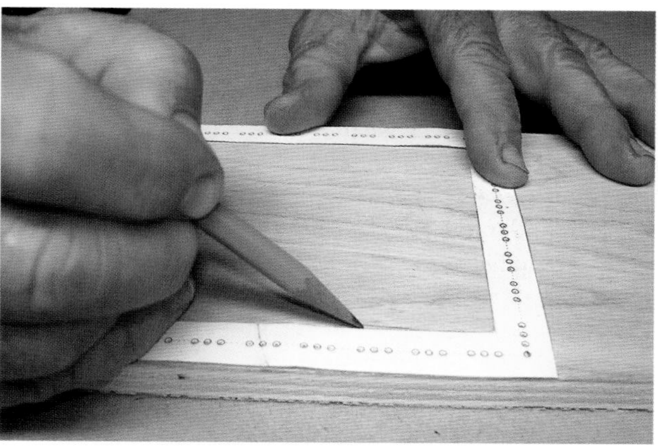

4. Place the photocopy of the template on the frame and use a pencil to mark the center cutout.

5. Clamp the frame to a tabletop or other rigid surface. Drill pilot holes at two opposite corners inside the pattern marks to give you somewhere to start your saw.

6. Use a saber saw or hand coping saw to cut out the center.
7. Now cut the frame to the right length. Leave it clamped down to do this if you use a handsaw.

8. Use a sanding block to smooth the loom frame and round the corners.
9. Lay the template on the frame and drive a couple of small finish nails in at the corners to hold it in place.
10. Use a larger nail with a sharp point to mark each pin location, tapping it lightly with the hammer to make a small hole. Remove the template once all the pin locations are marked.

11. Prepare the pins. Use wire cutters to cut the music wire into 1⅛"–1¼" lengths. Or if using needles, use pliers to break the eyes off.

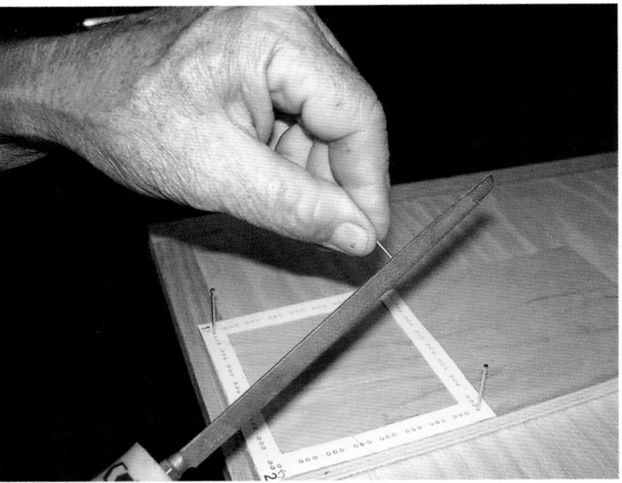

12. File one end of each pin flat, removing any rough parts so the pins won't snag the yarn when you weave.

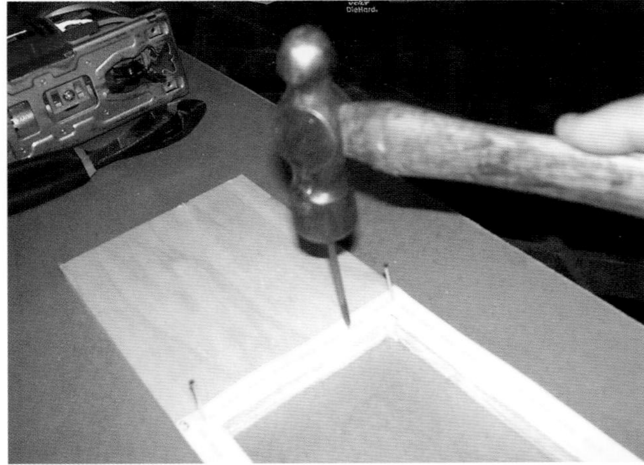

13. Use a small hammer to set a pin at each spot you marked in step 10.
14. Label the loom with the numbers 1, 2, and 3, and the corresponding arrows, as shown on the template.

2" x 2" template

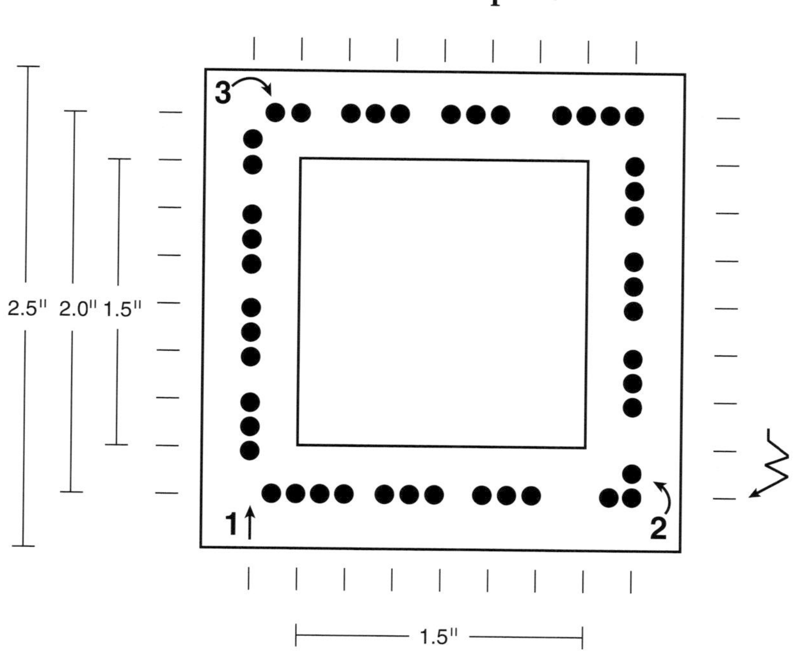

2" x 4" template

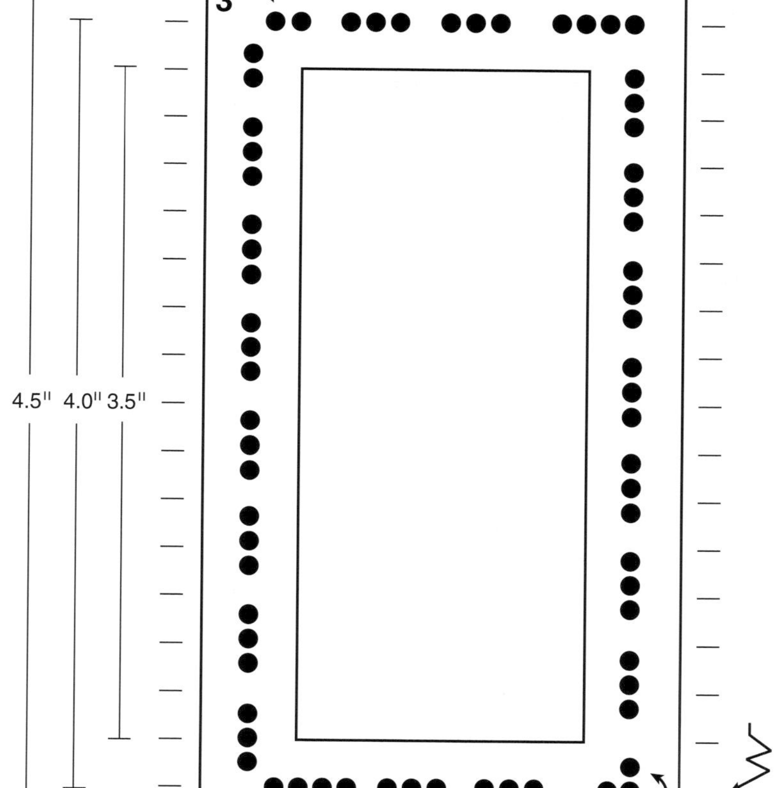

4" x 4" template

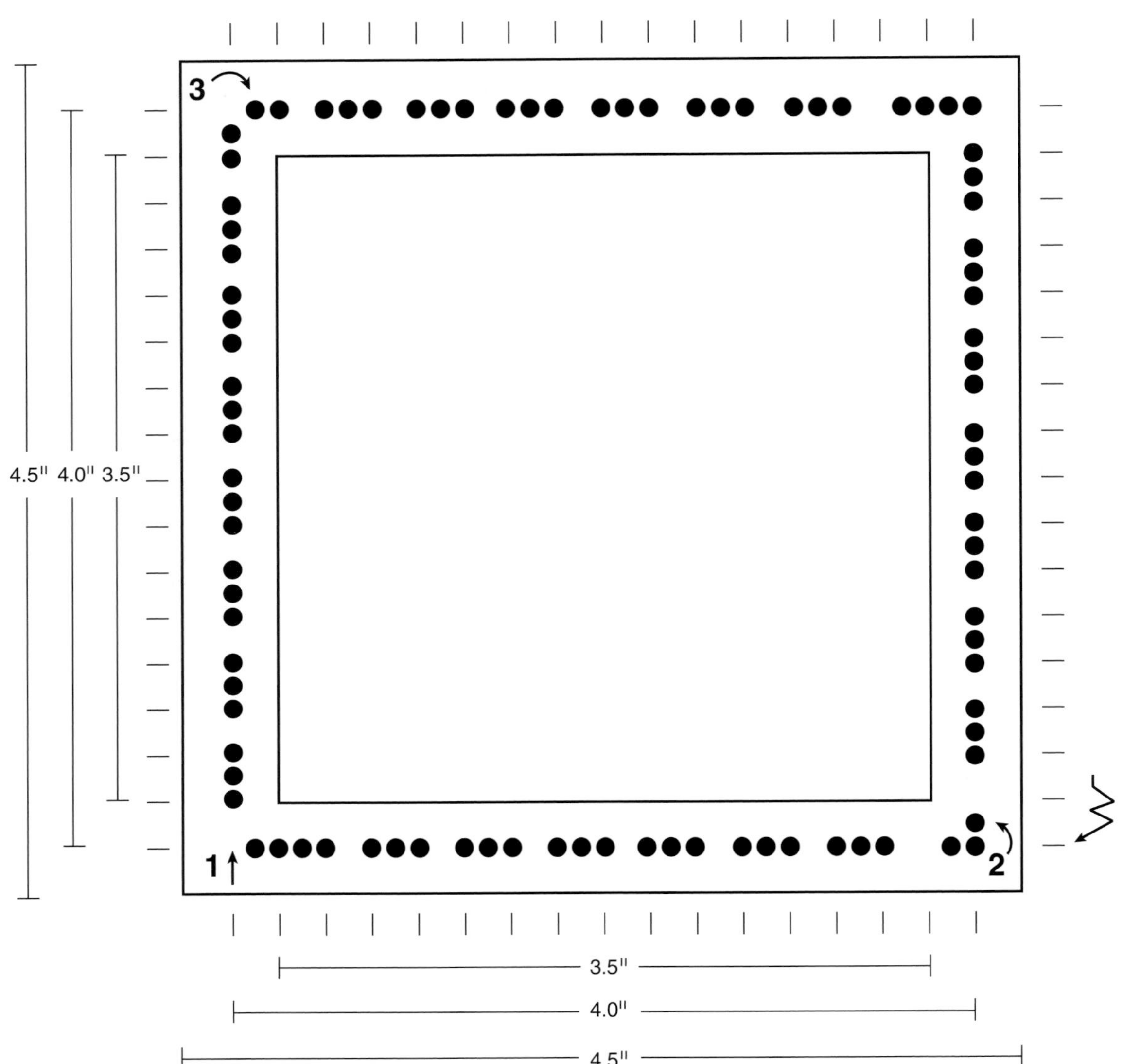

4" x 6" template

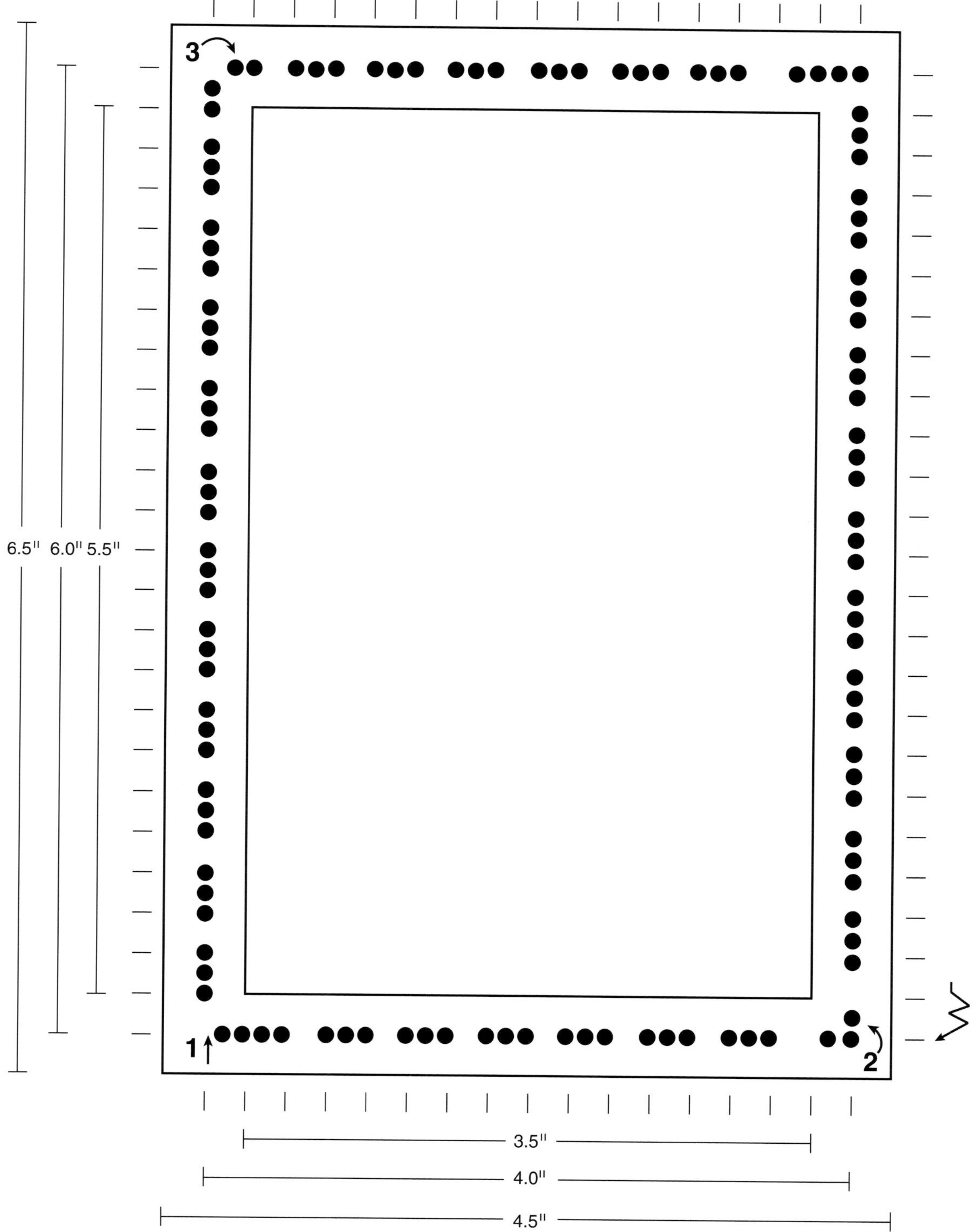

6" x 6" template

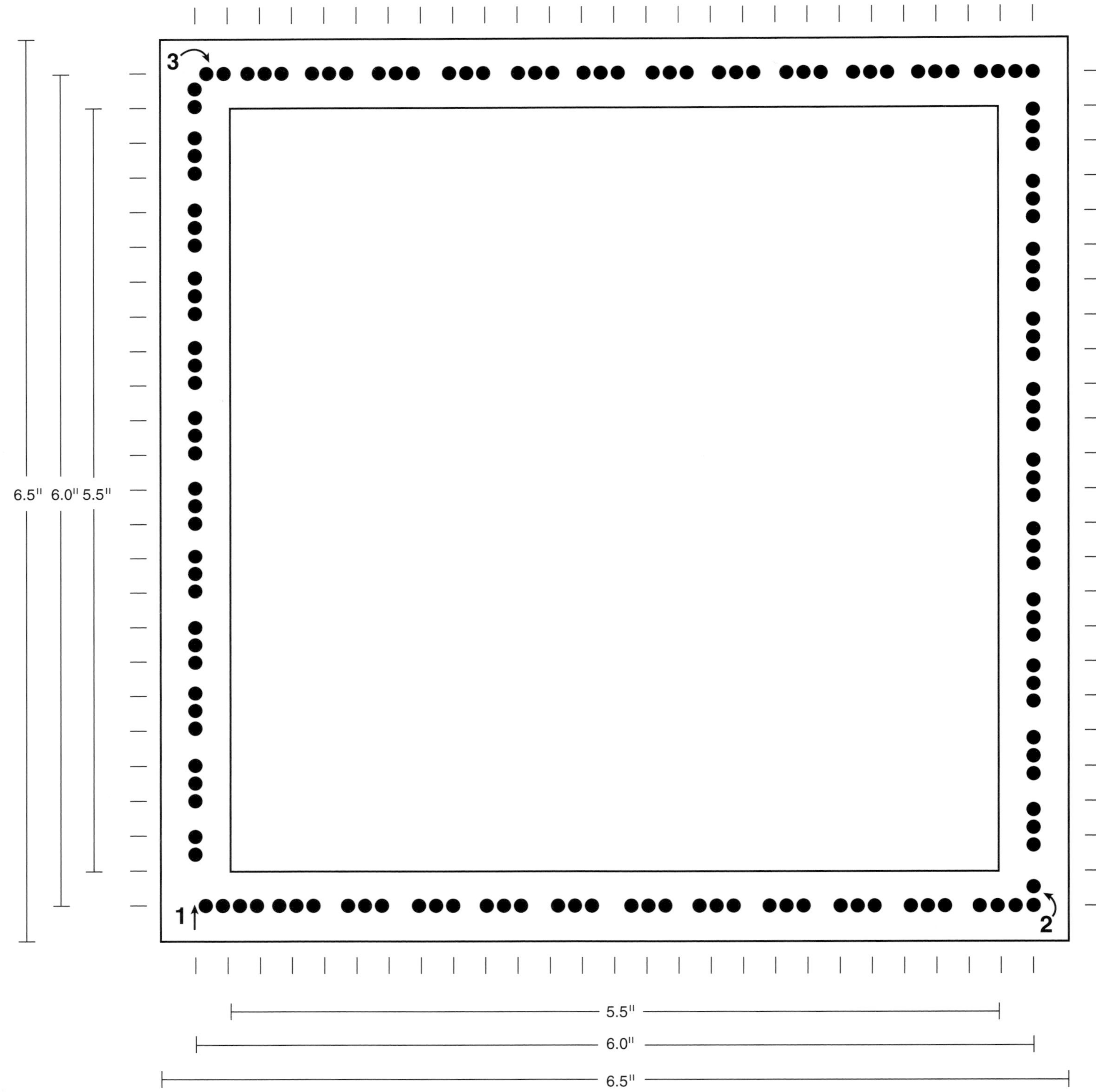

Projects Especially for the Zoom Loom

The Zoom Loom is a versatile update of the traditional pin loom. The following patterns all work very well with the Zoom Loom.

In each of these patterns, most of the work is done with a 4" x 4" loom. A few of the patterns suggest other sizes of weavies to use used for edging, stabilizing, and other purposes, but 4" x 4" weavies can easily be substituted.

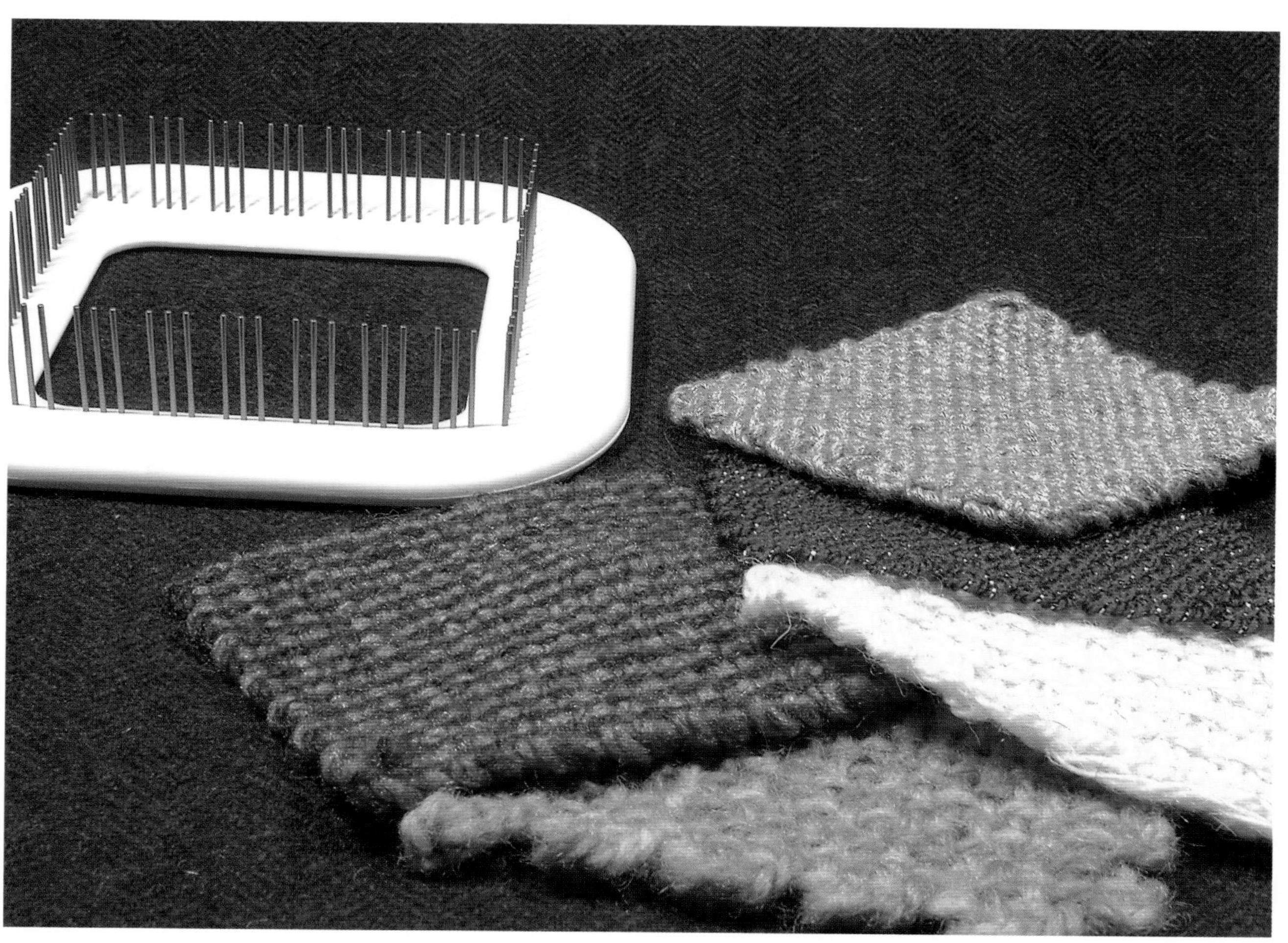

Yarn

Pin looms can handle a surprisingly large variety of yarns, from very thin to very thick. The looms are strong; you can weave with anything that will fit on the loom. The patterns in this book most often call for a medium-weight single-ply or 4-ply worsted yarn. Your choice of yarn should correspond to how you plan to use the weavie. If you are making a large, heavy-duty yarn bag, you may want to use a stronger, cheaper yarn. If you are making a toy or blanket for a child, you may want to use a yarn that is soft and easily washable. When planning for a project, buy extra yarn to allow for sampling and unforeseen problems, such as knots and defects in the yarn.

The pin loom's tiny size means that you can use it to work with small amounts of special yarn. The yarn market is bursting with new combinations of fibers and incredible textures and colors of hand-spun, hand-dyed yarns. A pin loom allows you to create with these beautiful yarns with very little waste.

How to Determine the Amount of Yarn You Need

The table below gives the approximate amount of yarn needed to create weavies of different sizes. If you add a single crochet edge to the square for joining it to another square, you will need slightly more yarn.

Size	Amount of Yarn Needed for a Square	For a Square with a Single Crochet Edge
2" x 2"	2 yd. (1.8 m)	3 yd. (2.7 m)
2" x 4"	4 yd. (3.7 m)	5.5 yd. (5 m)
2" x 6"	6 yd. (5.5 m)	7.5 yd. (6.9 m)
4" x 4"	7.5 yd. (6.9 m)	10 yd. (9.1 m)
4" x 6"	11 yd. (10 m)	15 yd. (13.7 m)
6" x 6"	16.25 yd. (14.9 m)	21 yd. (19.2 m)

Here is a general guideline for the amount of yarn needed for crochet edging or joining:

Single crochet: every 12" (30 cm) of sc = 8 ft. (2.4 m) of yarn
every 1 yd. (0.9 m) of sc = 8 yd. (7.3 m) of yarn

Half double crochet:
every 12" (30 cm) of hdc = 4 yd. (3.7 m) of yarn

Weaving Instructions for the Pin Loom

These directions demonstrate the process of winding the yarn and weaving on a 2" x 2" loom. All of the pin looms use the same pattern of pins and create the same cloth. The 2" x 2" loom is the smallest and easiest to practice on at first. The process is the same for the other sizes of looms—just with more pins. You can also find helpful video demonstrations of pin loom weaving online, on the Schacht website or on YouTube.

Directions

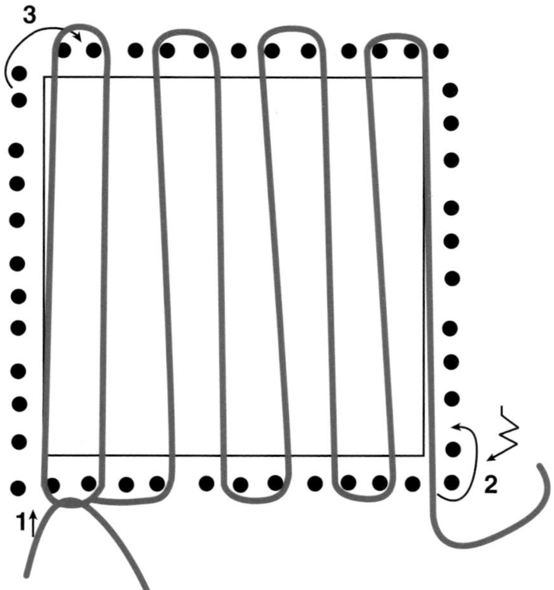

1. Hold the loom with the side marked with the 1 at the bottom. Loop the yarn around the first two pins at the top and bottom and either tie it off in a double knot or drape the end down to the left (after you complete the weaving, you will run the yarn back into the woven material). Take the working yarn around the second two pins at the bottom and then run it between the first and second pins in the cluster of three at the top. Continue to wind the yarn from top to bottom, always moving to the right, passing the yarn between the first and second pins in each cluster, as shown above.

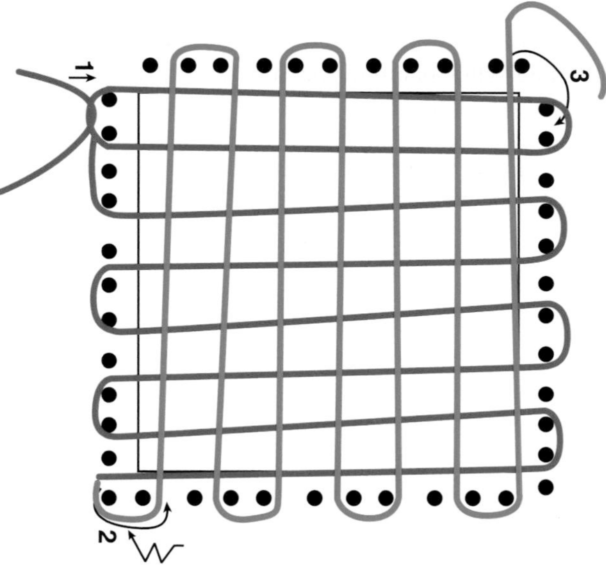

2. When you get to the number 2, follow the arrow around the corner. Turn the loom so that the 2 is on the lower left and continue the same pattern of winding the yarn around the pins, passing the yarn between the first and second pin in each cluster, until you come to number 3.

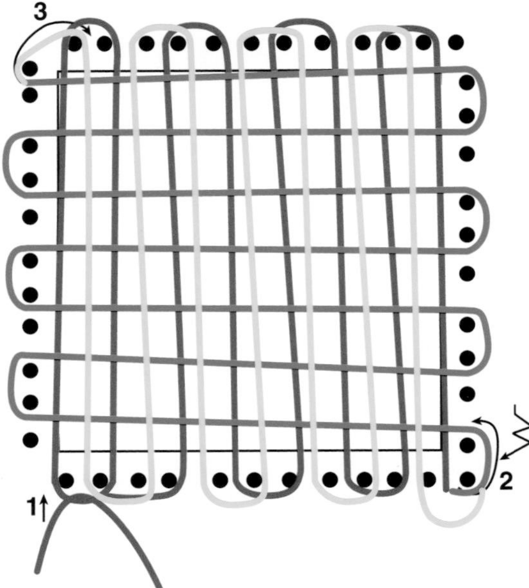

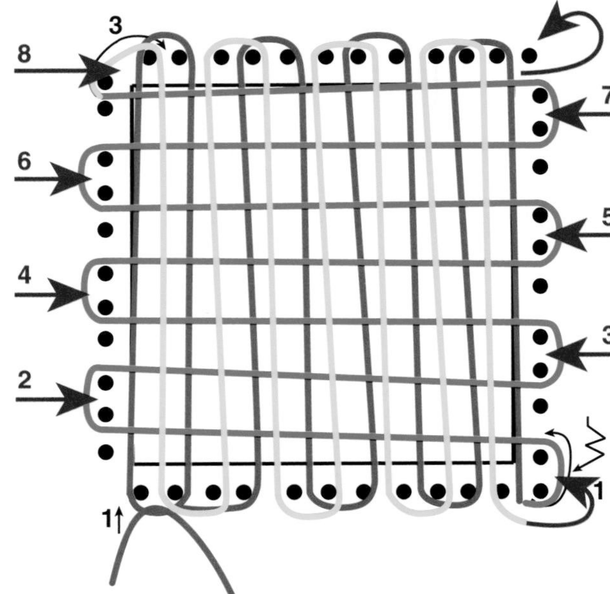

3. Turn the loom so that the side with the 1 is down again. Follow the number 3 arrow to pass the yarn between the two pins on the top left and then down around the middle two pins in the cluster of four. This sets up a different pattern. Now instead of passing the yarn between the first two pins in the clusters of three, you will wind it around the first two pins and pass it between the second pin and the third pin. This offsets the yarn from the layer below it. Continue winding across the loom, bringing the yarn around the first two pins in each cluster and between the second and third pins until you come back to the corner that has the W for "weave."

   Now your loom is ready to weave.
4. Measure out the amount of yarn you need to weave the square. For the 2" x 2" loom, you can do this by winding the yarn all the way around the outside of the loom 3 times. Each size of loom takes a different number of turns around the outside of the loom to measure off the yarn (see the box below). Unwind the yarn from around the loom and thread the end of the yarn onto a 3¾" (9.5 cm) weaving needle.
5. Now it's time to start weaving. Figure 4 shows where you should begin each line of weaving. You always start to weave between the pins where the yarn loops out, going over that outward loop. Be particularly careful with the first and last lines of weaving. It is easy to miss them, but if you do, you will find that you have a line of yarn that has not been woven in and falls away from the cloth.
6. After you weave through the last line, you will find that there is still one pin uncovered. Loop the yarn around that last pin to tie it off, then weave the yarn end into the completed cloth and cut off the excess. If you left the end of the yarn hanging at the beginning, weave it into the cloth at this time as well.

   You've completed one weavie!

Each loom takes a different length of yarn to complete the weave. This is measured by circling the yarn around the outside of the loom after you have completed winding the three layers on the pins.

2" x 2" loom	**3 times**
2" x 4" loom	**3.5 times**
2" x 6" loom	**5.5 times**
4" x 4" loom	**4.5 times**
4" x 6" loom	**5.5 times**
6" x 6" loom	**7 times**

Weaving Patterns

In the basic instructions for weaving you were told to weave over and under the threads alternately; this produces a plain weave, also called "tabby." Skipping some threads while weaving produces a pattern in the weave. Several of the projects call for woven-in patterns. The instructions for these patterns are given here.

Heart Pattern

For the 4" x 4" loom; used in the Sweetheart Baby Blanket and Bonnet.

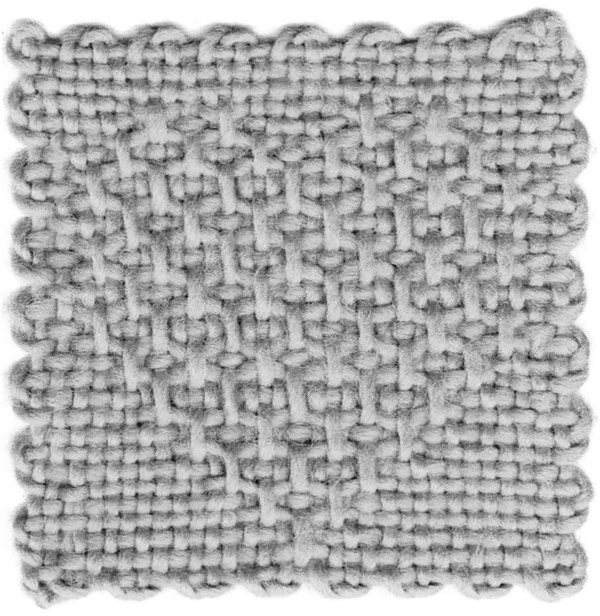

Row 1: Weave plain.
Row 2: Weave plain.
Row 3: W6, U3, O1, U3, W5, U3, O1, U3, W6.
Row 4: W4, U3, O1, U3, O1, U3, O1, U3, O1, U3, O1, U3, W4.
Row 5: W2, U3, O1, U3, O1, U3, O1, U3, O1, U3, O1, U3, O1, U3, W2.
Row 6: Same as row 4.
Row 7: Same as row 5.
Row 8: Same as row 4.
Row 9: Same as row 5.
Row 10: Same as row 4.
Row 11: W6, U3, O1, U3, O1, U3, O1, U3, O1, U3, W6.
Row 12: W8, U3, O1, U3, O1, U3, O1, U3, W8.
Row 13: W10, U3, O1, U3, O1, U3, W10.
Row 14: W12, U3, O1, U3, W12.
Row 15: W14, U3, W14.
Row 16: Weave plain.

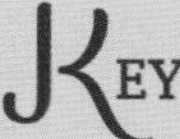EY

W = weave—this means to go under or over the strands of yarn in the normal (plain weave) manner for a certain number of threads
O = go over the number of threads specified
U = go under the number of threads specified

Eight-Rib Pattern

For the 4" x 4" or 4" x 6" loom; used in the Animals Toddler Blanket and Old-Fashioned Dishcloths.

Row 1: Weave plain.
Row 2: U3, O1, U3, O1, U3, O1, U3, O1, U3, O1, U3, O1, U3, O1, U3.
Row 3: W1, O3, W1, O3, W1, O3, W1, O3, W1, O3, W1, O3, W1, O3, W3.
Row 4 and all even rows: Same as row 2.
Row 5 and all odd rows: Same as row 3.
Last row: Weave plain.

Crossroad Pattern

For the 4" x 4" loom; used in the Monk's Bag.

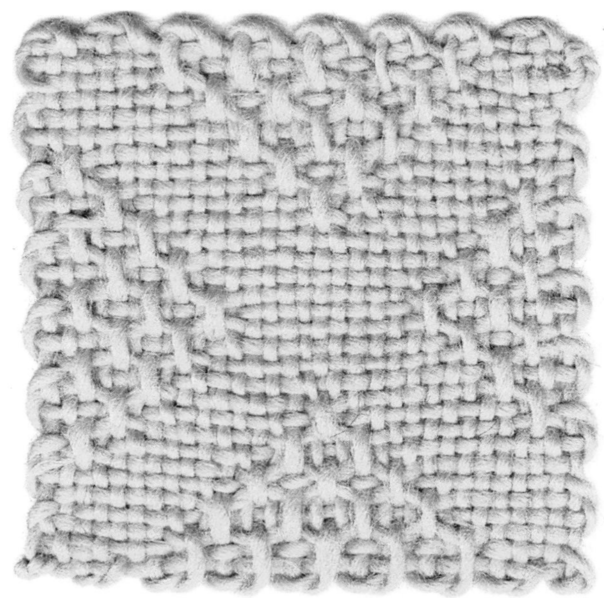

Row 1: Weave plain.
Row 2: W8, U3, O1, U3, O1, U3, O1, U3, W8.
Row 3: W10, U3, O1, U3, O1, U3, W10.
Row 4: U3, W9, U3, O1, U3, W9, U3.
Row 5: W2, U3, W9, U3, W9, U3, W2.
Row 6: U3, O1, U3, W17, U3, O1, U3.
Row 7: W2, U3, O1, U3, W13, U3, O1, U3, W2.
Row 8: U3, O1, U3, O1, U3, W9, U3, O1, U3, O1, U3.
Row 9: W2, U3, O1, U3, W13, U3, O1, U3, W2.
Row 10: U3, O1, U3, W17, U3, O1, U3.
Row 11: W2, U3, W9, U3, W9, U3, W2.
Row 12: U3, W9, U3, O1, U3, W9, U3.
Row 13: W10, U3, O1, U3, O1, U3, W10.
Row 14: W8, U3, O1, U3, O1, U3, O1, U3, W8.
Row 15: W6, U3, O1, U3, O1, U3, O1, U3, O1, U3, W6.
Row 16: Weave plain.

Triple-Rib Pattern

For the 4" x 4" loom; used in the Lace Bag.

"Pass through" means to take the needle through on the same path as the previous woven line without weaving.

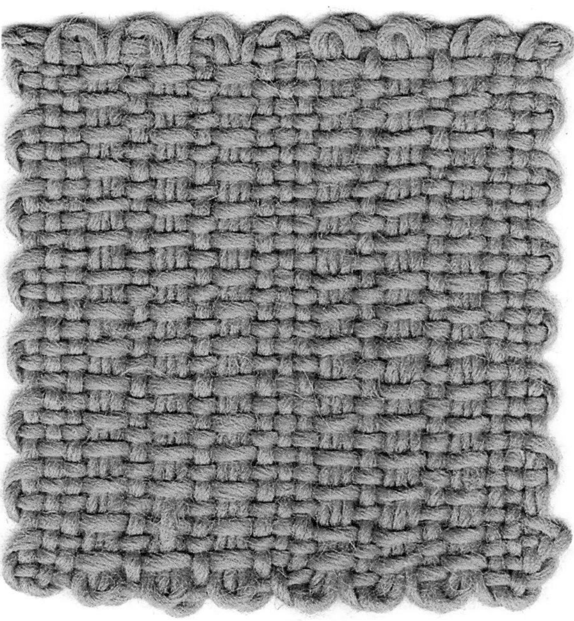

Row 1: Weave plain.
Row 2: Weave plain.
Row 3: Pass through.
Row 4: Weave plain.
Row 5: Pass through.
Row 6: Weave plain.
Row 7: Pass through.
Row 8: Weave plain.
Row 9: Weave plain.
Row 10: Pass through.
Row 11: Weave plain.
Row 12: Pass through.
Row 13: Weave plain.
Row 14: Pass through.
Row 15: Weave plain.
Row 16: Weave plain.

Five-Star Pattern

For the 4" x 4" loom; used in the Blessing Path Toddler Blanket.

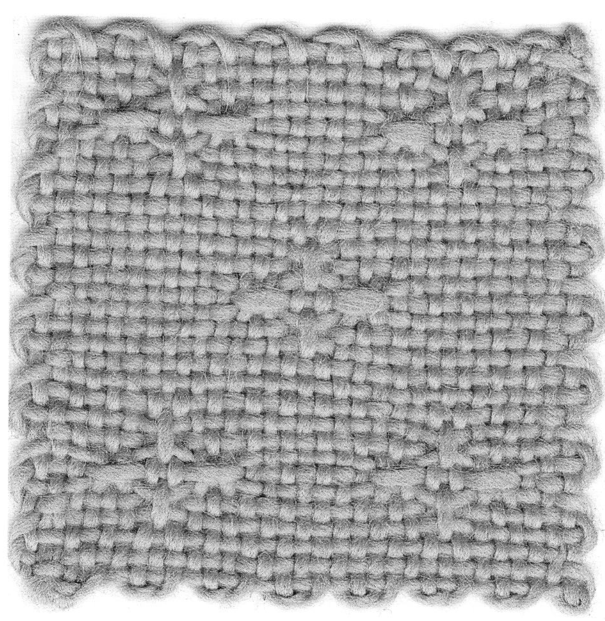

Row 1: Weave plain.
Row 2: Weave plain.
Row 3: W6, U3, W13, U3, W6.
Row 4: W3, O3, W3, O3, W7, O3, W3, O3, W3.
Row 5: W6, U3, W13, U3, W6.
Row 6: Weave plain.
Row 7: Weave plain.
Row 8: W14, U3, W14.
Row 9: W11, O3, W3, O3, W11.
Row 10: W14, U3, W14.
Row 11: Weave plain.
Row 12: Weave plain.
Row 13: W6, U3, W13, U3, W6.
Row 14: W3, O3, W3, O3, W7, O3, W3, O3, W3.
Row 15: W6, U3, W13, U3, W6.
Row 16: Weave plain.

One-Star Pattern

For the 4" x 4" loom; used in the Blessing Path Toddler Blanket.

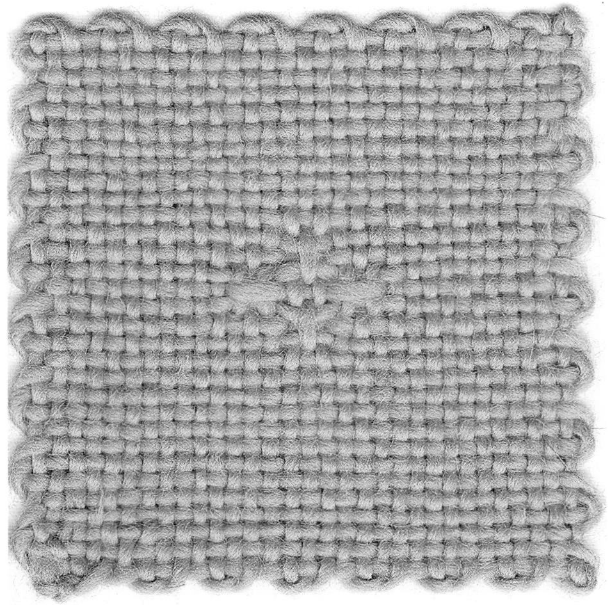

Row 1: Weave plain.
Row 2: Weave plain.
Row 3: Weave plain.
Row 4: Weave plain.
Row 5: Weave plain.
Row 6: Weave plain.
Row 7: Weave plain.
Row 8: W14, U3, W14.
Row 9: W11, O3, W3, O3, W11.
Row 10: W14, U3, W14.
Row 11: Weave plain.
Row 12: Weave plain.
Row 13: Weave plain.
Row 14: Weave plain.
Row 15: Weave plain.
Row 16: Weave plain.

Six-Star Pattern

For the 4" x 6" loom; used in the Regency-Style Reticule.

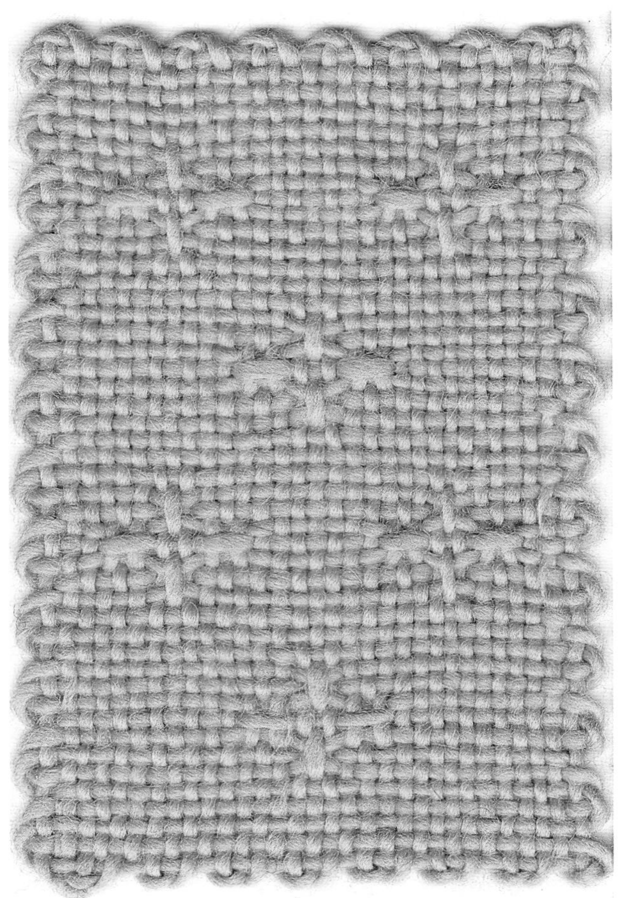

Row 1: Weave plain.
Row 2: Weave plain.
Row 3: Weave plain.
Row 4: W14, U3, W14.
Row 5: W11, O3, W3, O3, W11.
Row 6: W14, U3, W14.
Row 7: Weave plain.
Row 8: Weave plain.
Row 9: W6, U3, W13, U3, W6.
Row 10: W3, O3, W3, O3, W7, O3, W3, O3, W3.
Row 11: W6, U3, W13, U3, W6.
Row 12: Weave plain.
Row 13: Weave plain.
Row 14: W14, U3, W14.
Row 15: W11, O3, W3, O3, W11.
Row 16: W14, U3, W14.
Row 17: Weave plain.
Row 18: Weave plain.
Row 19: W6, U3, W13, U3, W6.
Row 20: W3, O3, W3, O3, W7, O3, W3, O3, W3.
Row 21: W6, U3, W13, U3, W6.
Row 22: Weave plain.
Row 23: Weave plain.
Row 24: Weave plain.

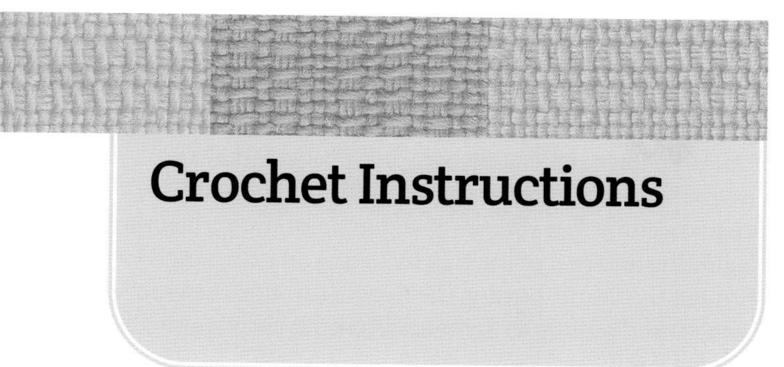

Crochet Instructions

Everything in this book is made out of pin loom weavies. However, you will often be instructed to use some basic crochet techniques to join the weavies together and to add some finishing touches. Instructions for the stitches you need are given here; if you find you need more help, there are hundreds of videos online that demonstrate these techniques.

Joining the Yarn

Start by making a slip knot: Make a loop in the yarn, then pull the end of the yarn connected to the skein or ball (called the working yarn) through the loop. Pull to tighten. This produces an adjustable loop with a knot at the base.

To join the yarn and start crocheting along the edge of a weavie, insert the crochet hook into the fabric where you want to start, place the slip knot on the hook, and pull the slip knot through the fabric. Wrap the yarn around your hook once ("yarn over") and pull the yarn through the slip knot. Pull to tighten. Your yarn is joined securely and you are ready to start crocheting.

Chain (ch)

Starting with a loop on your hook, wrap the working yarn around your hook once (yarn over), and pull this yarn through the original loop to create a new loop.

Slip Stitch (sl st)

You can use slip stitches to create a neat join between the beginning and end of a round of crochet, or you can work them across the surface of a piece to create a line of stitches. In either case, the stitch is worked the same: Insert the crochet hook into the fabric or stitch where instructed, yarn over, and pull the yarn up through the fabric and through the loop already on your hook. Sl st completed.

Single Crochet (sc)

Insert the hook into the loop or stitch. Yarn over and pull up a loop (2 loops on hook). Yarn over and pull the yarn through both loops (1 loop on hook). Sc completed.

Half Double Crochet (hdc)

Yarn over, then insert the hook into the loop or stitch. Yarn over and pull up a loop (3 loops on hook). Yarn over and pull the yarn through all 3 loops (1 loop on hook). Hdc completed.

Double Crochet (dc)

Yarn over, then insert the hook into the loop or stitch. Yarn over and pull up a loop (3 loops on hook). Yarn over and pull the yarn through the first 2 loops (2 loops on hook). Yarn over again and pull the yarn through the remaining 2 loops (1 loop on hook). Dc completed.

Fastening Off

To fasten off crochet securely so it doesn't unravel, cut the yarn, leaving a short tail (1" to 2" [2.5 to 5 cm]). Pull the tail through the loop on your hook and pull to tighten the knot.

Working Around the Edge of a Piece

To add a crochet edge to a piece, join the yarn in the middle of any side as described above. Crochet around the edge of the weavie, working one stitch in each loop. At each corner, work one stitch in the first corner loop, chain 2, then work another stitch in the second loop of the same corner. When you get all the way around the piece to where you started, finish off the crochet edge by working a slip stitch in the top of the first stitch of the round. Cut the yarn, pull the end through the loop, and pull tight to fasten off.

Crochet Abbreviations

ch = chain
dc = double crochet
hdc = half double crochet
sc = single crochet
sl st = slip stitch

Joining Instructions

Mattress Stitch

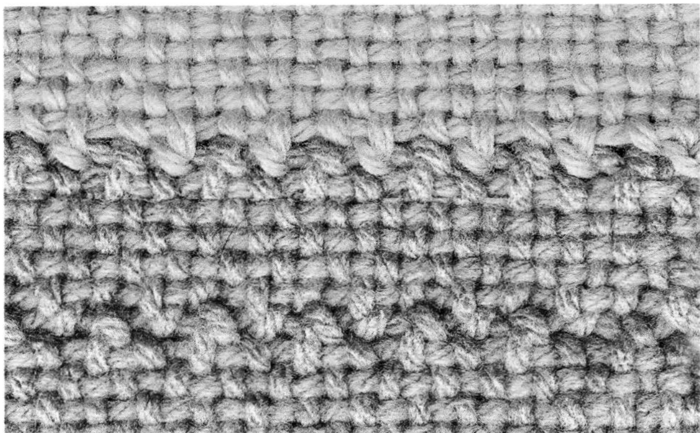

The mattress stitch is a quick joining method. This method is used in the Sweetheart Baby Blanket and Blessing Path Toddler Blanket.

The first step when using this join is to check the squares and make certain that they are all facing the same direction with the corners matching. If you know you will be using this stitch, you might consider stacking the squares as you weave them to keep them oriented with the same side up. Each corner of the weavie is slightly different, so you will be able to match them up by looking closely.

To join two squares together, line them up facing the same way and then flip one over onto the other. You will notice that the side loops are not lying on top of one another; they alternate between the two squares. Using your weaving needle, weave the yarn back and forth between the two squares as shown in the diagram. If you are just joining two squares together, knot the yarn at the beginning and end of the join by taking an extra stitch through the fabric, putting the needle through the loop formed, and pulling to tighten. Weave the yarn ends back through the fabric.

To join several squares together into a blanket, start by laying out all the squares for the project (all facing the same way). You will begin by joining the weavies in vertical strips, and then join the strips together.

Starting at the top, flip the top square over onto the second square. Join the squares as described above. Do not tie off the yarn, but leave several inches hanging on both sides of the seam. After completing the join, open the squares up and pull firmly to help straighten and flatten out the stitching. Then take these two attached squares and flip them down over square number 3 and repeat the joining process. Don't forget to leave several inches of yarn on each side of the strip; you will need this when you start joining the strips together. Continue flipping and joining squares until the project is in a series of strips.

Flip the first strip over onto the second. Take the hanging pieces of yarn that meet at each join and double knot them together, running the ends back into the fabric. This ensures that the corners will all fit snugly together, without holes.

Once all the corners are joined, work the mattress stitch down the edge of the strips in the same way as before. After joining the strips, open them up and pull firmly to flatten out the seam.

It is likely that sooner or later you will run into squares where the loops on the two squares lie directly over one another rather than alternating between squares. You will have to slide one square just a bit to one side in order to keep the same look. Fortunately, there is a lot of give in the weaving and you can tug it all back into place as you go along.

The mattress stitch gets a big plus for speed of execution: Using a long needle, you can weave through all or most of the loops before pulling the yarn through. It gets a minus for strength because the join is dependent on the single piece of yarn that is being woven through. It is best for projects made with lightweight yarn or small projects in which the stitching will not be under much stress.

Double Overcast Stitch

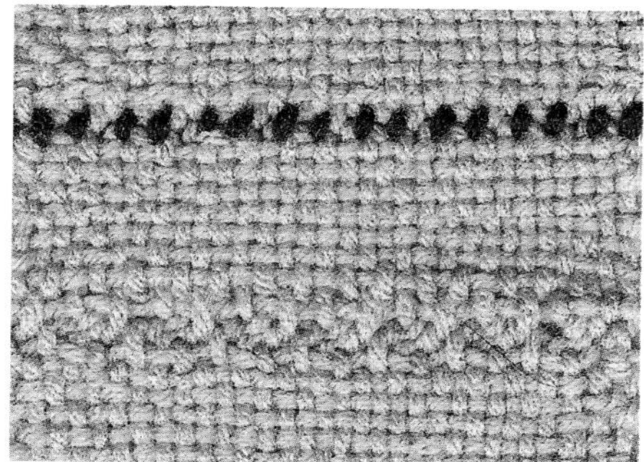

The double overcast stitch is much stronger stitch than the mattress stitch and it is really difficult to undo. It lies quite flat and even on the top side, with a slight but discernible ridge on the back. This stitch is used in the Animals Toddler Blanket and the Monk's Bag.

To join two squares together with this stitch, line up the squares so that the loops lie on top of one another rather than alternating. Using a tapestry needle, lead the joining yarn through the matching corner loops and then take another stitch back through the same two loops to make a double overcast stitch. Go through each set of loops two times, pulling the yarn snug. Tie off at the beginning and end of the seam by taking an extra stitch through the fabric, putting your needle through the loop formed, and pulling tight to fasten off. Weave the yarn ends back through the fabric so they cannot be seen.

To join a number of squares into a larger piece, join them first into strips, then join the strips together. As with the mattress stitch, do not tie off the yarn at the beginning and end of each join, but leave several inches of yarn loose on each side of each join when you make the strips; before you join the strips together, use these ends to line up the strips of cloth and close the corners.

Although it is easiest to do when the loops match exactly, you can still use the double overcast stitch if the loops are off from one another. Just make sure that you don't skip any loops. After completing the join, open the squares up and pull firmly to help straighten and flatten out the stitching.

A word of warning: Because this seam is different on the front and back, it is important to check and make sure you are sewing each seam on the correct side. When you are sewing the squares in a "closed" position and then opening and flattening them to make the strip, it is easy to get the material turned around and end up with some flat seams and some ridged ones.

Single Crochet Join

Single crochet makes a fast, easy, and strong join. Lay the two weavies together, preferably with loops matching, and single crochet through the loops of both layers. The crochet stitch will produce a pronounced ridge on one side and therefore works best in projects where the ridge doesn't matter or you can use it to your advantage. You can see it on several of the cactus plants, the old-fashioned dishcloths, the small bags, and the hobo bag. The crochet seam gives extra texture and can be worked in a contrasting color, adding to the design.

Single Crochet Edge Whipstitched Together

This method is a little more laborious, but it is also the most useful of the joining methods. It is very strong and lends extra weight and texture to your piece as well as giving it a good, long-lasting finish.

Add a single crochet edge to each weavie, using the same color yarn that was used to make the weavie so that the crochet edge will be more contiguous with the woven cloth. Make sure that you crochet through each loop and chain two at each corner so that the weavie will lie flat. The corners are each a little different, but this is a very forgiving process.

Lay out the weavies according to the pattern and whipstitch them together through the crochet edges, always going into the fabric from the same side and coming out the other side and then around the edge to go in from the front again for the next stitch (see diagram). If the crochet loops don't quite add up, you can take a double stitch in one of them.

The color of the yarn to use for the whipstitching is determined by the pattern. If you are joining two different-colored blocks and want to highlight one of the blocks, use the other color for the whipstitching.

Whipstitching

When assembling projects with this method, it is important that the squares align, with all corners coming neatly together. Unlike the other joining methods, which call for connecting the squares in long strips and then stitching the strips together, with this method, you should assemble the weavies in blocks, so that you will end up attaching, for example, one four-by-four grouping of squares to another four-by-four grouping.

Diagonal Join with a Single Crochet Edge

This technique is used to create a square with two different colors meeting diagonally. Start with two woven squares of the same size. Sew them together on the diagonal using a running stitch (a simple in-and-out stitch straight across the fabric). Fold open the piece so that there are two same-color triangles on either side of the diagonal seam. Single crochet around the square, changing colors at the seam so that each half is edged in its own color.

Blanket Stitch

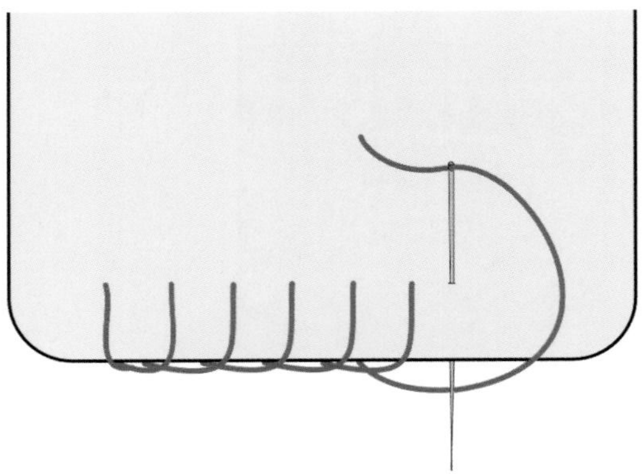

The blanket stitch is used in these patterns to secure one layer of fabric (such as a pocket) on top of another layer of fabric, usually using contrasting yarn as a decorative element. Work this stitch from left to right, as shown in the diagram. Stitch through both layers of fabric, always going in from the same side and coming out on the same side, as with whipstitch—but before you pull each stitch tight, take the needle through the loop of yarn. This stitch creates a visible line of contrasting yarn along the edge of the fabric.

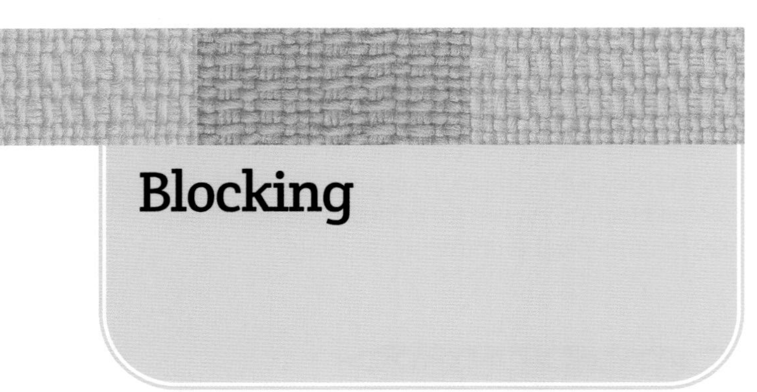

Blocking

Blocking is a process of flattening and straightening out your weaving or crochet. Many pin loom products, especially the 3-D projects, do not need to be blocked. However, blocking can give blankets and other flat projects a more finished appearance, and it is essential when dealing with crochet purse straps. The process shapes and sets the design and smoothes the stitches into place. There are different ways to block, but for the projects in this book I recommend steam blocking.

You'll need a steam iron, cotton towels, and a hard surface like a counter or table to block on. Be sure to pad and protect these surfaces from moisture with a layer of cotton rugs or towels.

Start by laying the item facedown on the blocking surface and pulling it into its proper shape with your fingers or rustproof pins. Set your iron on the heat setting appropriate for the fiber type and, holding it just above the project, steam the piece thoroughly. If the project is very delicate, use a light cotton towel over the item as a steaming cloth and very lightly steam the project through the cloth.

In the case of a purse strap, lay a portion of it flat on the blocking surface and work the steam slowly along the length, shaping and flattening as you go. Take care not to touch the iron to the project because this can flatten the stitches too much or scorch the yarn. Leave the item in place until it's cool.

TIP: **You should always check the yarn label for any special care instructions before you steam block a project. Lots of natural fibers, such as cotton, linen, and wool, respond well to steam blocking. Many acrylics and some blends need to be handled with care because too much heat or steam could melt them. If you're unsure about blocking your project, try blocking a single weavie made with the same yarn first to see how much heat you can use and what the result will be.**

CHAPTER TWO

Bags and Cases

Small Bags

If you are new to working with pin looms, consider making a few small bags to start. You get the thrill of creating a very handy little purse or gift bag with some ease. A small bag is fun and impressive with minimal effort.

The directions below show you how to make two small bags, but there are many possibilities. Try a different pin loom size or joining approach to create a unique bag, purse, or pouch.

Finished Measurements

4" x 4" (10 x 10 cm)

Tools

- 4" x 4" pin loom
- 4" x 6" pin loom
- Size G-6 (4.0 mm) crochet hook
- Tapestry needle

Yarn

Small Bag #1

- 20 yd. (18 m) variegated medium worsted (weight category 4) chenille yarn
- 6 yd. (5.5 m) solid dark blue medium worsted (weight category 4) acrylic yarn

Small Bag #2

- 20 yd. (18 m) variegated red/gold fine (weight category 2) sparkle yarn (acrylic and metallic polyester blend)
- 1 ft. (30 cm) yellow medium worsted (weight category 4) wool-acrylic blend yarn

Notions

- 1" (2.5 cm) button

Instructions

Small Bag #1

1. Weave:
   - One 4" x 6" weavie
   - One 4" x 4" weavie
2. Stack the weavies together with the loops on one end matching. Single crochet around the edges of the two weavies with dark blue.
3. Single crochet around the edge of the larger weavie where it extends beyond the other (the lip and flap of bag) with dark blue.
4. Chain 48" in the variegated chenille yarn for a purse strap. Whipstitch each end of the strap to the outside of the bag.
5. Attach ornamental button in the middle of the bag.
6. Chain 4" to form a button loop. Attach to the inside of the flap above the button. Weave in all ends.

Small Bag #2

1. Weave two 4" x 4" weavies.
2. Stack the weavies together so that the loops match and single crochet through both layers around three sides. Turn bag inside out.
3. Double crochet around the top edge.
4. Cut about 24" of the yellow yarn and fold it in half. Weave the doubled length of yarn through the row of double crochet, going over or under every two crochet stitches. Knot the ends of the yellow yarn to use as pull strings.
5. Chain 16" of red yarn for a handle. Sew the ends together, then attach the loop to the inside of the bag near one seam. Weave in all ends.

NOTE: **Keep in mind that the even weave produced by your pin loom makes a perfect ground for all types of decoration. Consider adding beads, fringe, stitching, or other embellishment to your small bag.**

Flash Drive Holder

We end up carrying all sorts of electronic equipment these days and some of them, like flash drives, are getting smaller and more difficult to keep track of. This flash drive holder is intended as a pretty and inexpensive way to tuck away anything that is small and precious to you. Because it's not very big, this is a great project for utilizing small amounts of special yarn.

Once you get started with a small item like a flash drive holder, you may find yourself weaving all sorts of cell phone and tablet holders. For more ideas, take a look at the tablet case on page 27. You may also notice that the Weaving Kit (page 34) is another iteration of this same design, using much the same approach for joining the pieces.

I have been using the regular size flash drive holder for several years. I keep it tucked in the zipped pocket of my purse and have never found a need for a fastener, such as ties or Velcro, to keep it closed. Since its pockets face inward, nothing can slip out.

Finished Measurements

Regular: 2" x 8" (5 x 20 cm)
Mini: 2" x 4" (5 x 10 cm)

Tools

- 2" x 4" pin loom
- 2" x 2" pin loom (mini size only)
- Size G-6 (4.0 mm) crochet hook
- Tapestry needle

Yarn

Main color: Bulky (weight category 5) variegated yarn
Accent colors: Medium worsted (weight category 4) yarn

Regular Flash Drive Holder

- 11 yd. (10 m) main color
- 4 yd. (3.7 m) each of two accent colors

Mini Flash Drive Holder

- 6 yd. (5.5 m) main color
- 2 yd. (1.9 m) each of two accent colors

Notions

- Velcro strip for closure (optional)
- Split ring or carabiner to attach to purse (optional)

Instructions

Regular Flash Drive Holder

1. Weave two 2" x 4" weavies in the main color for the outside of the holder. Weave two 2" x 4" weavies in coordinating colors for the pockets.
2. Use the main color and the single crochet join to attach the pockets to the base. Crochet around the outside edge of the piece, attaching three outer sides of the pockets to the cover, while leaving the inside edge of each pocket open.
3. Fold the piece in half, with the pockets to the inside.
4. If desired, sew the Velcro strips on the inside edges of the opening to close the flash drive holder.
5. Sew the split ring or carabiner to the outside of the middle fold. Weave in all ends.

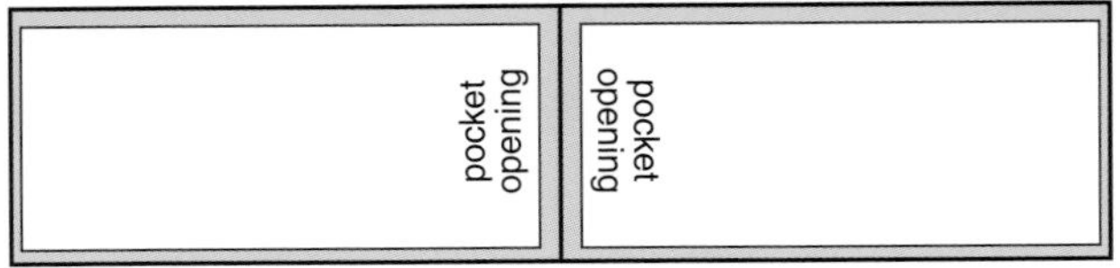

Mini Flash Drive Holder

1. Weave one 2" x 4" weavie in the main color for the outside of the holder. Weave two 2" x 2" weavies in coordinating colors for the pockets.
2. Use the main color and the single crochet join to attach the pockets to the base. Crochet around the outside edge of the cover, attaching three outer sides of the pockets to the base and leaving the inside edge of each pocket open.
3. Fold the piece in half with the pockets to the inside.
4. If desired, sew the Velcro strips on the inside edges of the opening to close the flash drive holder.
5. Sew the split ring or carabiner to the outside of the middle fold. Weave in all ends.

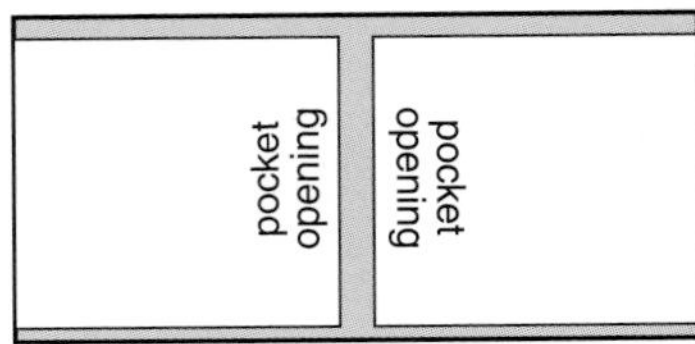

TIP: **This project uses a lot of 2" x 4" weavies. If you can't find or don't want to buy or make a loom in this size, remember that you can get the same thing with a 2" x 2" loom. Just make two 2" x 2" weavies for every 2" x 4" weavie the directions call for.**

Tablet Case

The tablet case shown here was constructed especially for my Samsung tablet and it has worked great—no scratches or dents in the tablet since I started using it! In addition, the case is nice to hold on to and it has a pen/stylus pocket built in just the way I want it. The great thing about working with your own looms is that you can make a case that is just right for you—and, of course, for the people you care enough about to weave a special case for.

The basic design can be easily customized to match your favorite device. I have included diagrams for a tablet case with the opening on a narrow end, like a manila envelope. I have also included diagrams for some smaller tablets. Whether you use one of my diagrams or create your own, be sure to try it out with the tablet before you do your final stitching.

Finished Measurements

12" x 8" (30 x 20 cm)

Tools

- 2" x 2" pin loom
- 4" x 4" pin loom
- 4" x 6" pin loom
- Size G-6 (4.0 mm) crochet hook
- Tapestry needle

Yarn

Medium worsted (weight category 4) yarn

- 130 yd. (119 m) rough-spun wool yarn in main color
- 18 yd. (16 m) single-ply wool-mohair blend yarn in accent color

Notions

- 1" (2.5 cm) or larger button

Instructions

The directions given here are for the Samsung tablet case. If you are making a different variation, the number of weavies required and the specific arrangement of the weavies will be different, but the basic process is the same.

1. Weave:
   - Fifteen 4" x 4" weavies
   - One 4" x 6" weavie
   - One 2" x 2" weavie
2. Join the 4" x 4" squares in a three-by-five grid using the mattress stitch.
3. Double-check that the case will fit the tablet, then fold a three-by-two section up to complete the case. Sew this section in place with the mattress stitch.
4. Dog-ear the two outside weavies on the flap to the inside and stitch the edges down to complete the envelope look.
5. Place the 2" x 2" weavie in the middle of the inside of the flap and sew it in place. This serves as reinforcement for the button and tie string.
6. Using accent yarn, single crochet around the flap and the opening of the case.
7. Single crochet across one 4" side of the 4" x 6" weavie with the accent yarn.
8. Position the 4" x 6" weavie on the front of the bag. I placed the pocket at an angle to keep the pens from falling out. Crochet it in place using slip stitch in accent yarn. Use slip stitch to work two straight lines through both the pocket and the layer below for dividers.
9. Using the accent yarn, work a 36" to 40" chain and tie a knot in one end. Tack the other end of the chain to the top of the flap, over the reinforced area. Sew the button on top of the chain, winding the thread around the button a number of times to make a strong thread shank (to leave space for the string tie) before tying off. Weave in all ends.

VARIATION

If you don't have a 4" x 6" loom, you can get a little creative with the pockets. Here are a couple of ideas:

- **Option 1: Weave two 4" x 4" squares, one for pens and one for miscellaneous items, and have two pockets on the front.**
- **Option 2: Weave two 4" x 4" weavies and join them with mattress stitch. If an 8" (20 cm) pocket feels too deep, you could overlap the weavies or turn the edge under 1" (2.5 cm) or so.**

VARIATION

If you want more of the "manila business envelope" look, follow the diagram on the next page. This calls for one less 4" x 4" square. You will join the squares in a two-by-seven grid, folding the cloth up lengthwise to form a bag with only two squares in the flap.

Regular Tablet Case

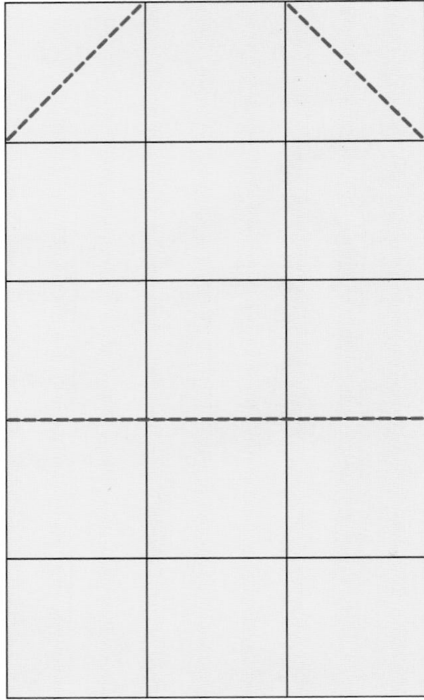

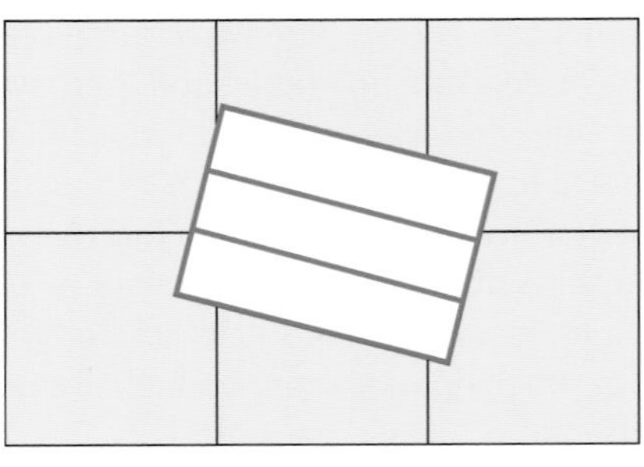

front

Manila Envelope Variation

(8" x 12" [20 x 30 cm])
Yarn needed: 116 yd. (106 m)

front

iPad Case

(12" x 8½" [30 x 22 cm])
Yarn needed: 113 yd. (103 m)

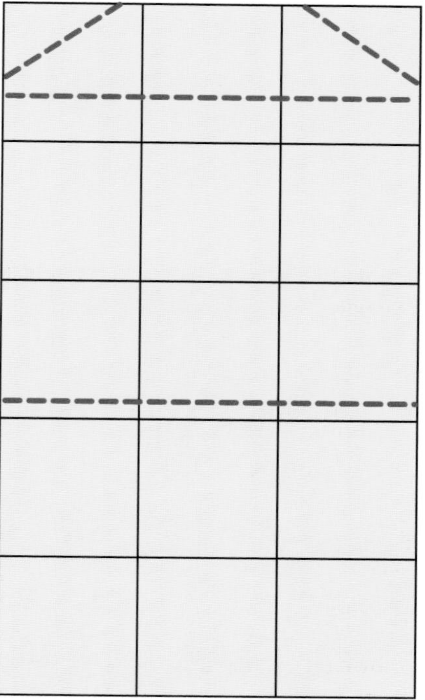

Kindle Fire Case

(8" x 10" [20 x 25 cm])
Yarn needed: 90 yd. (82 m)

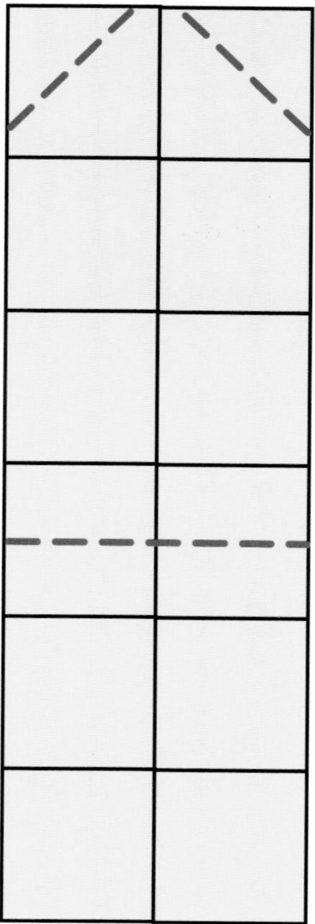

Kindle HD Case

(7" x 10" [18 x 25 cm])
Yarn needed: 75 yd. (69 m)

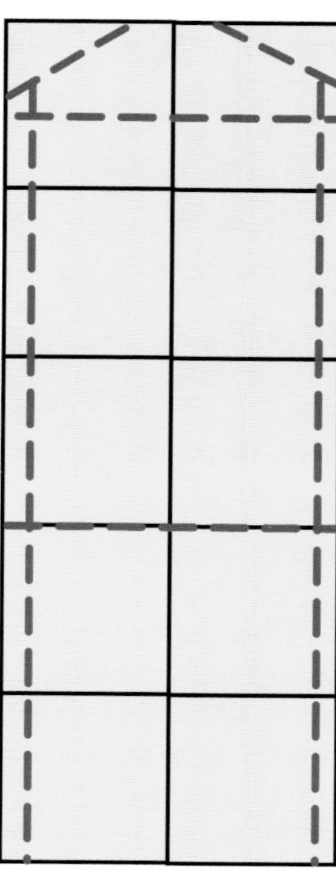

Yarn Bag

Any weaver or crocheter needs a good yarn tote—or several! This project is a great way to use up all the experimental weavies you may have tucked away in your craft closet. The dimensions of the bag are easy to adjust to your needs; just add a few more rows of weavies for an even bigger, more colorful bag.

Yarn bags make great storage. Make several in colors coordinated to your decor. Hang them on Shaker pegs for a creative storage solution.

Finished Measurements

Approximately 18" x 12" x 2" (45 x 30 x 5 cm)

Tools

- 4" x 4" pin loom
- 2" x 4" pin loom
- 4" x 6" pin loom
- Size G-6 (4.0 mm) crochet hook
- Tapestry needle

Yarn

Medium worsted (weight category 4) acrylic and wool-acrylic blend yarn

- 190 yd. (174 m) dark blue
- 40 yd. (37 m) moss green
- 40 yd. (37 m) turquoise
- 20 yd. (18 m) pale blue
- 20 yd. (18 m) medium blue
- 20 yd. (18 m) light aqua
- 10 yd. (9 m) bronze
- 20 yd. (18 m) coral
- 20 yd. (18 m) pink

Notions

- Two 16" (40 cm) dowel-type purse handles, ½" (1.2 cm) in diameter

Instructions

1. Weave the following 4" x 4" squares:
  - Ten dark blue weavies
  - Four moss green weavies
  - Four turquoise weavies
  - Two pale blue weavies
  - Two medium blue weavies
  - Two light aqua weavies
  - One bronze weavie
  - Two coral weavies
  - Two pink weavies

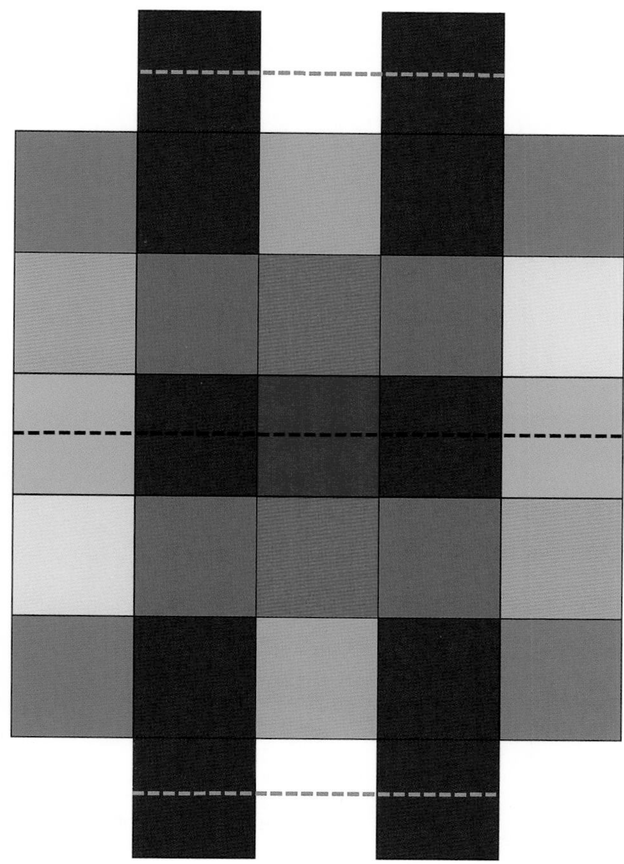

2. Single crochet around the edge of each square in its own color, then whipstitch the squares together as shown in the diagram.

3. Fold the piece formed in half and whipstitch sides together with dark blue yarn to form a bag.

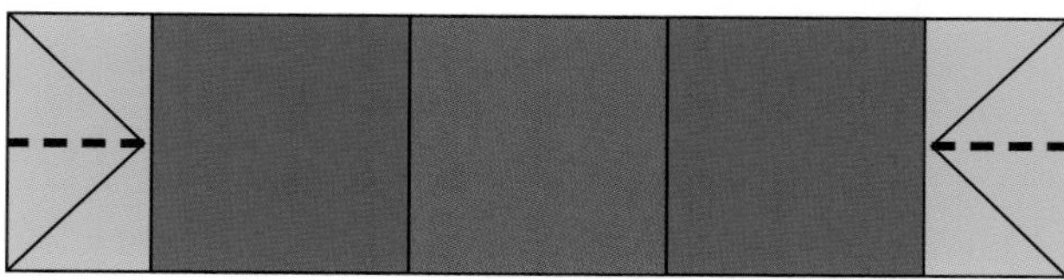

4. Turn in the bottom corners and tack down to make a flat bottom, as shown in the diagram above.

5. Loop the blue weavies that extend beyond the top edge of the bag around the handles and stitch in place. Weave in all ends.

Lace Bag

The light "lace" layer of this bag is woven using the triple-rib pattern and is highlighted by the contrast with the dark squares underneath. This gives the bag a sense of lightness and dazzle without sacrificing function.

Finished Measurements

8" x 8" (20 x 20 cm)

Tools

- 4" x 4" pin loom
- Size G-6 (4.0 mm) crochet hook
- Tapestry needle

Yarn

- 85 yd. (78 m) silver-gray fine (weight category 2) acrylic and metallic polyester yarn
- 69 yd. (63 m) charcoal medium worsted (weight category 4) wool yarn

Sample made with Vanna's Glamour by Lion Brand and 100% virgin wool yarn in deep charcoal.

NOTES: This is a multi-use pattern. This size bag is great for cosmetics or other small items, but the size can be easily varied. Consider making an even smaller bag from three 4" x 4" squares, which would give you a 4" x 6" bag, or making one out of two 4" x 4" squares—just big enough for a tiny purse or a special gift bag. The Lace Bag will dazzle when made with any color of fine, sparkly yarn over a heavier, contrasting yarn.

Instructions

1. Weave:
   - Eight squares with the metalic yarn using the triple-rib pattern (see page 17)
   - Nine squares with the dark yarn in plain weave
2. Place a lace square on top of a plain square with the loops matching and join them by single crocheting around the edge in the fine yarn. Repeat for the other 8 lightweight squares.
3. Whipstitch the squares together into a piece two blocks wide by four blocks long.
4. Fold the piece in half, with the lace to the outside, and whipstitch the two sides closed.
5. Turn the bag inside out and stitch the remaining plain weave square to the middle of one side to serve as an inner pocket.
6. Half double crochet around the top edge of the bag with the fine yarn.
7. Crochet a chain 24" long. Using the tapestry needle, weave the chain around the top edge, going through every other opening between half double crochet stitches.
8. Sew the two ends of the chain to the inside of the bag on one side, allowing the chain loop to extend off of the other side. Close the bag by tightening the drawstring. Weave in all ends.

Weaving Kit

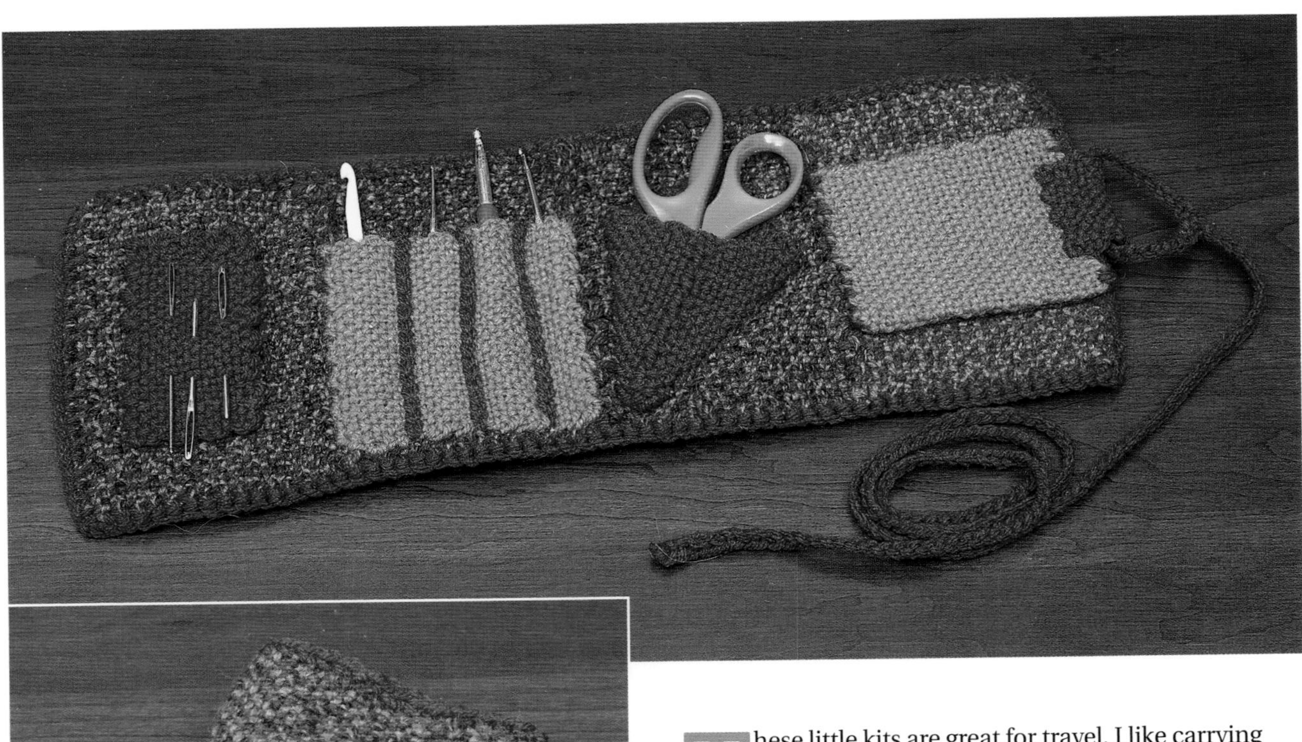

These little kits are great for travel. I like carrying all my hooks and needles and scissors in a secure, non-clanking case when I am on the road. Kits like this also make great gifts for fellow weavers. I have called it a weaving kit, but it works equally well for crochet or sewing tools and notions.

The kit is designed to be closed with a string tie. It is easy to use and very low-tech. You can add a Velcro strip to hold it closed if you choose—but the upside of the string tie is that no matter how much you place in the kit, you can always tie it closed.

Finished Measurements

15" x 6" (38 x 15 cm)

Tools

- 2" x 2" pin loom
- 4" x 4" pin loom
- 2" x 4" pin loom
- 4" x 6" pin loom
- Size G-6 (4.0 mm) crochet hook
- Tapestry needle

Yarn

- 32 yd. (30 m) variegated bulky (weighty category 5) acrylic yarn (sample made with Lion Brand Tweed Stripes in Mixed Berries)
- 44 yd. (40 m) burgundy medium worsted (weight category 4) acrylic yarn
- 15 yd. (14 m) coral medium worsted (weight category 4) acrylic yarn

Notions

- ½" x 2" (1.2 x 5 cm) Velcro strip (optional)

Instructions

1. Weave:
   - Four 4" x 6" mixed variegated and solid weavies (wind with variegated yarn and weave with solid)
   - One 4" x 4" burgundy weavie
   - One 2" x 4" burgundy weavie
   - One 2" x 2" burgundy weavie
   - Two 4" x 4" coral weavies
2. Join the long edges of the four 4" x 6" weavies together using mattress stitch to form a long strip for the base.
3. Edge the piece created with single crochet in burgundy (remembering to chain 2 at each corner).
4. Fold one 4" x 4" burgundy weavie into a cone shape (for the scissors) and stitch into place on the base.
5. Sew the bottom edge of a coral 4" x 4" weavie to the base along the dotted line in the diagram. Then fold the weavie up so that the pocket is about 3" (7.5 cm) tall, with a 1" (2.5 cm) fold at the bottom and sew the sides of the pocket to the base. This creates a pocket with a stronger bottom edge than if you just sewed it flat to the base.

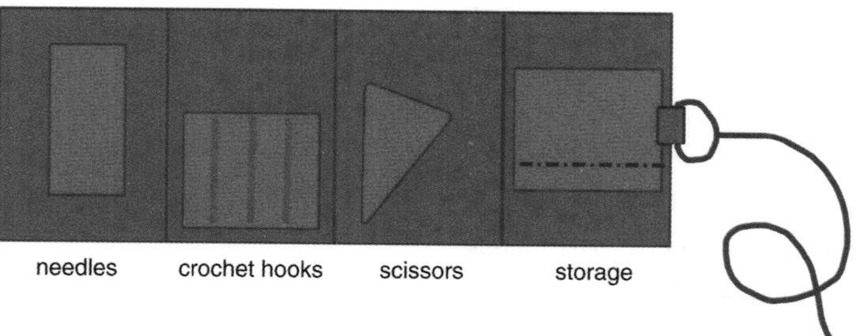

6. Sew the top edge of the 2" x 4" burgundy weavie to the base with burgundy yarn, leaving the other edges free. This creates a flap that you can stick needles into.
7. Sew the remaining 4" x 4" coral weavie to the second panel of the base with burgundy yarn around the sides and bottom edge. Work lines of slip stitch in burgundy yarn through this pocket to divide it into slots for pens or crochet hooks.
8. Wrap the 2" x 2" weavie around the right edge of the piece and sew it in place with burgundy yarn, going through all layers of fabric. Weave in all ends.
9. With the burgundy yarn, make a chain 36" long (do not fasten off yet). Thread the working end of the chain through the 2" x 2" weavie on the edge and slip stitch the end to a spot about 3" (7.5 cm) farther up, to create a loop around the weavie. Fasten off. Close the case by folding it in thirds, then wrap the chain around the whole thing several times and tuck the end under the wraps to hold it closed.

Variation

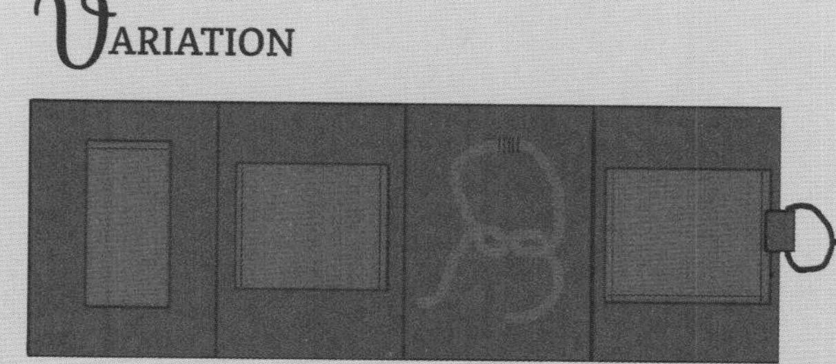

This project is easy to customize to carry whatever tools you want it to. You can also, with a little bit of tweaking, transform it into a great little jewelry case. The weavie on the first panel is sewed down on all four sides to attach hook earrings to; the next panel has a weavie left open on the ends to attach bracelets around. The third panel has a crochet chain to tie rings to, while the final one has a pocket with a Velcro closure at the top for miscellaneous small jewelry pieces. Use these customizations or try out your own to create the perfect case for your needs.

Crossbody Bag

This bag has a lining built in—light-colored weavies that are attached before assembling the bag. You can pick a lining color that complements the bag's color and style. This bag was designed with one exterior and one interior pocket, but feel free to add more—you could put a pocket on each of the 6" sides, inside and out.

Finished Measurements

Purse: 7" x 7" (18 x 18 cm)
Strap: 56" long (140 cm)

Tools

- 4" x 4" pin loom
- 2" x 6" pin loom
- 4" x 6" pin loom
- 6" x 6" pin loom
- Size G-6 (4.0 mm) crochet hook
- Tapestry needle

Yarn

Medium worsted (weight category 4) yarn

- 124 yd. (113 m) neutral-colored rough-spun wool yarn
- 15 yd. (14 m) maroon single-ply wool yarn
- 103 yd. (94 m) acrylic yarn for lining

Notions

- 1¼" or 1½" (3 or 4 cm) steel-colored purse rings
- Two ¾" (2 cm) silver buttons

TIP: **This project calls for a lot of different sizes of looms. Keep in mind that if you don't have the right size looms, you can join 2" x 2" weavies to get the dimensions you need. Or, if you are working solely with a 4" x 4" loom, you can change the dimensions of the project slightly to create an 8" x 8" bag. Use four joined squares for the wide surfaces. Fold the 4" x 4" squares for the sides in half and they will be self-lining. If you make changes, check the Yardage Requirement Table on page 12 for the amount of yarn you'll need.**

Instructions

1. For the exterior of the bag, weave:
   - Three 6" x 6" weavies
   - One 4" x 4" weavie
   - Three 2" x 6" weavies

   For the lining, weave:
   - Two 6" x 6" weavies
   - Four 2" x 6" weavies
   - One 4" x 6" weavie
   - Two 4" x 4" weavies
2. Lay two of the three 6" x 6" exterior weavies on top of the two 6" x 6" lining weavies, with the loops matching; lay the three exterior 2" x 6" weavies on the 2" x 6" lining weavies. Using the neutral yarn, join the exterior weavies and lining weavies together by single crocheting around the whole edge.
3. Lay the remaining 6" x 6" exterior weavie on top of the remaining 2" x 6" lining weavie and the 4" x 6" lining weavie so that there is a narrow opening between the two lining pieces. This will be the bag's front flap, and the opening will allow the flap to bend more easily over the front of the bag. Single crochet the pieces together using the neutral yarn.
4. Single crochet around one 4" x 4" lining weavie. Attach it to the lining side of one of the 6" x 6" weavies to serve as an interior pocket.
5. Following the diagram, whipstitch the lined weavies together. Fold the sides and front of the bag in to form the bag, and whipstitch.
6. Single crochet the exterior 4" x 4" weavie to the remaining 4" x 4" lining weavie. Place the lined square (to be used as a pocket) on the front of the bag and blanket stitch around the sides and bottom edge with the maroon yarn.
7. With maroon yarn, single crochet around the opening of the bag, continuing around the edge of the front flap.
8. Attach one of the two buttons close to the bottom of the exterior pocket, and attach the other on the front flap. Cut an 18" length of maroon yarn, double it over, put the top loop around the top button, and knot the yarn to the button. Tie a knot in the yarn every few inches to make the cord easier to grip. To close the bag, wind the knotted yarn in a figure-8 around the two buttons.
9. With the neutral yarn, chain approximately 60" (150 cm), or your prefered strap length. Turn and sc up the whole length of the chain. When you reach the end, turn again and sc up the bottom edge of the chain. This process makes a strap that is approximately ¾" (2 cm) wide with a trough running down the middle. Slip stitch a line of the maroon yarn along the length of the trough. Use a steam iron to soften and flatten the strap.
10. Sew purse rings to the sides of purse with maroon yarn. Sew the strap to the rings. Weave in all ends.

NOTE: **If you would like a wider strap, you can add more rows of single crochet on each edge. Experiment with a larger hook for a slightly looser, larger crochet loop.**

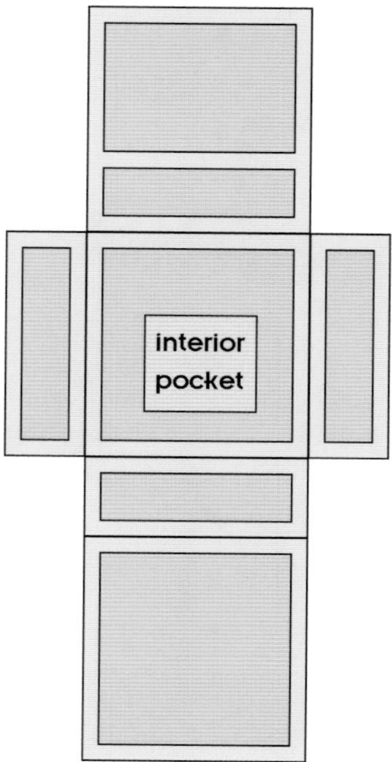

Light Shoulder Bag

This bag was woven from a hand-dyed wool-mohair-silk yarn. The color is luminous and is highlighted by the simple design. This purse is a little different in that the built-in pockets—a large one in the front and a small one in the back—open to the outside instead of to the inside of the purse.

Finished Measurements

8½" x 10½" (22 x 27 cm)

Tools

- 4" x 4" pin loom
- Size G-6 (4.0 mm) crochet hook
- Tapestry needle

Yarn

Medium worsted (weight category 4) yarn

- 97 yd. (89 m) variegated single-ply wool-mohair-silk yarn
- 140 yd. (128 m) coral wool-acrylic blend yarn for lining
- 55 yd. (50 m) red wool-acrylic blend yarn for joining

Notions

- Two pink floral buttons
- One dark coral flat button
- Three magnetic purse snaps
- Two 1" (2.5 cm) D rings

Instructions

1. Weave:
   - Twelve 4" x 4" squares in variegated yarn
   - Fourteen 4" x 4" squares in coral yarn
2. Stack a variegated square on a solid square and use single crochet to join them together using the red yarn. Repeat seven more times for a total of eight lined squares.
3. Fold the remaining four variegated 4" x 4" squares in half. Using the red yarn, single crochet around the three open sides. Do not crochet across the fold.
4. Whipstitch the lined squares and the half squares together as shown in the diagram. For the front, you will have a two-by-two block of squares (panel B) plus a separate block made of two half squares (A). For the back, you will have a block of two full squares (C) and a block of two full squares and two half squares (D).
5. With the red yarn, single crochet around the separate blocks (indicated by the red line in the diagram), but don't crochet across the lip of the purse (the folded edges of the half squares).
6. Single crochet around the six remaining lining squares with coral. Whipstitch four squares together in a two-by-two block using the same yarn. Whipstitch the other two squares together along one side. These pieces will be the two inside pockets.
7. Attach the two-by-two lining block you just made to panel B, whipstitching the edge of the lining piece to the inside of the crochet edging on panel B along the sides and bottom edge (leave the top open for the pocket opening). Whipstitch panel A to the top edge of the lining block, with the folded edge up.
8. Attach the smaller lining block from step 6 to panel C, whipstitching the edge of the lining piece to the inside of the crochet edging along the sides and bottom edge, leaving the top open. Whipstitch panel D to the top edge of the lining block, with the edge with the folded half squares up.
9. You have now built two pockets into the two sides of the bag. Add magnetic purse snaps to the pockets; cover the stitches on the outside with buttons. I used a rose button on the front closure and a flat orange button on the back closure.

Variation

If you are using a soft or lightweight yarn for the lining, you may wish to reinforce the liner before attaching the magnetic snap. Weave two 4" x 4" or 2" x 2" squares in the red yarn and stitch them to the back of the liner pieces for reinforcement.

10. With the red yarn, whipstitch the two halves of the bag together at the bottom. Fold the two halves of the bag together and whipstitch along each side.
11. Attach the D rings to the sides of the bag with red yarn.
12. With the red yarn, chain approximately 60" (or your prefered strap length). Turn and sc up the whole length of the chain. When you reach the end, turn again and sc up the bottom edge of the chain. This process makes a strap that is approximately ¾" wide with a trough running down the middle. Slip stitch a line of the variegated yarn along the length of the trough. Use a steam iron to soften and flatten the strap.
13. Sew the strap onto the D rings. Weave in all ends.

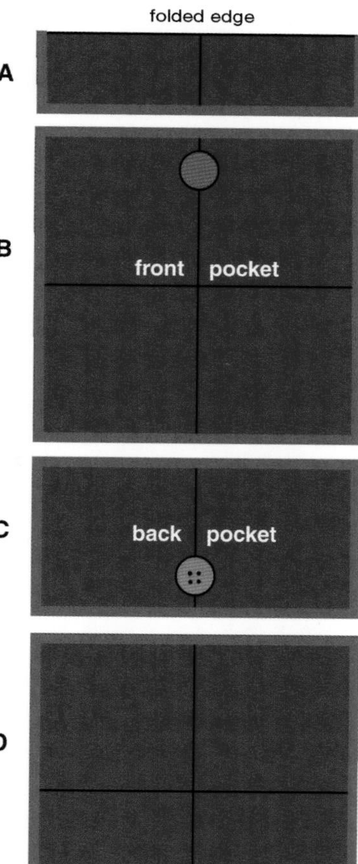

Monk's Bag

This pattern is based on the traditional Buddhist monk's bag. These bags are used to carry all of the monks' worldly possessions and exemplify the ideal of a life of simplicity. I worked to maintain the same simplicity and style in these woven versions. A popular embellishment on the traditional monk's bag is the eternal knot, which represents the intertwining of wisdom and compassion. The X in the crossroad pattern found in the bodies of the bags represents this eternal knot.

This bag has three variations. The largest is made with a panel of nine 4" x 4" squares on the front and back with an edging of three squares on each side that continue into the strap. The squares of the front panel are all woven with the crossroad pattern. I used a single-ply wool yarn for these squares, which gives them a very rich, textured look.

The medium bag is made with a panel of four 4" x 4" squares in the front and back, as well as a cover flap of four more squares. When I designed this bag, I wanted to contrast the richly colored, single-ply middle panel with a homespun edge. There is no crochet edging on this bag in order to highlight the woven strap.

The small Monk's Bag is just one woven square in front and back with 2" x 4" weavies for the sides and strap. I made the smallest one just because it was so cute, not thinking that it would be particularly useful. However, I have had a number of friend's daughters who thought this one was the best, just big enough for a cell phone.

Before you assemble your bag, check the strap length. Depending upon your height, you may want to add a few more squares so that you have a comfortable cross-body strap.

If you are going to carry pointed or heavy objects in your Monk's Bag, you may want to line it. There are a number of popular methods for lining a bag, including a sewn-in cloth lining and an inner layer of duct tape. Both approaches will increase the amount of weight that you can comfortably carry without overextending the bag. You can find multiple approaches to lining your bag online. My personal favorite is the duct tape. It is extremely strong and long-lasting, there is no sewing with tiny little needles involved, and you can choose a fabulous color to match your bag.

Finished Measurements

Large Bag: 16" x 12" (40 x 30 cm)
Medium Bag (with flap): 12" x 8" (30 x 20 cm)
Small Bag: 6" x 4" (15 x 10 cm)
Straps for all three bags: 40" to 48" long (100 to 120 cm)

Tools

- 4" x 4" pin loom
- Size G-6 (4.0 mm) crochet hook
- Tapestry needle

Yarn

Medium worsted (weight category 4) wool and wool-blend yarn

Large Monk's Bag
- 150 yd. (137 m) deep wine
- 150 yd. (137 m) amber
- 30 yd. (27 m) gold

Medium Monk's Bag
- 110 yd. (100 m) turquoise
- 100 yd. (91 m) light gray heather

Small Monk's Bag
- 36 yd. (33 m) gold
- 48 yd. (44 m) teal

Notions

Large Monk's Bag
- 2 buttons, approximately 1" (2.5 cm) in diameter
- Magnetic purse snap (optional)

Medium Monk's Bag
- 2 buttons, approximately 1" (2.5 cm) in diameter (optional)

Small Monk's Bag
- 1 button, approximately 1" (2.5 cm) in diameter (optional)

Instructions

Large Monk's Bag

1. Weave:
    - Eighteen 4" x 4" squares in wine using the crossroad pattern (see page 16)
    - Sixteen to eighteen 4" x 4" gold squares in plain weave
2. Using the double overcast stitch, sew nine of the wine-colored squares together into a square panel. Single crochet around panel in same yarn. Repeat to make a second panel of nine wine-colored squares. Whipstitch the two panels together along one side.
3. Sew the gold squares together into a strip using the double overcast stitch. This is a good time to check the length of the strip against your height in order to get a comfortable length. Single crochet around the edge of the strip. Folding the gold strip in two widthwise, whipstitch the two sides of the gold strip to the front and back panels. Whipstitch the bottom end of the gold strip closed.
4. Using the gold accent yarn, single crochet along the top of the front panel and around the entire edge of the strap. Repeat on the back panel and the other edge of the strap.
5. Attach the magnetic purse snap to the inside top edges of the panels and sew buttons on the front and back, over the snap. Weave in all ends.

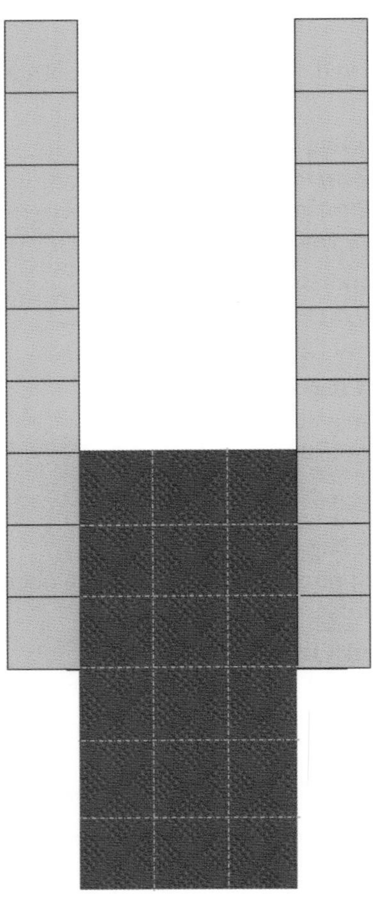

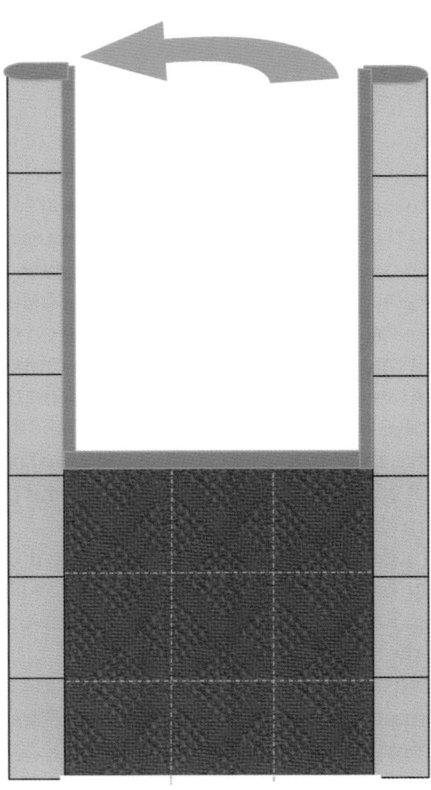

VARIATION

If you prefer to just use the buttons for closing the purse, make a 6" chain of wine-colored yarn and attach it under one button. Wind this tie around the buttons to close the bag.

Medium Monk's Bag

1. Weave:

- Twelve 4" x 4" squares in turquoise using the cross-road pattern (see page 16)
- Six 4" x 4" squares in light gray heather in plain weave
- Ten to twelve 2" x 4" weavies in light gray heather in plain weave

If you don't have a 2" x 4" loom, keep in mind that 2" x 2" weavies can be substituted. Just double the number of weavies needed.

2. Use the double overcast stitch to sew four of the turquoise squares together into a square panel. Single crochet around the panel in the same color. Make two more panels of four turquoise squares. Whipstitch the three panels together into a wide strip.

3. Make two strips of three 4" x 4" light heather squares using the double overcast stitch. Sew all the 2" x 4" light heather weavies together into a strip and attach one 4" x 4" strip at each end. Fold in the corners of the 4" x 4" square as shown in the diagram and stitch in place.

4. With turquoise yarn, single crochet along the edges of the two 4" x 4" squares at each end of the light heather strip; single crochet along the bottom of each strip with light heather yarn. Using turquoise yarn, whipstitch the two long sides of the strip to two of the square panels, leaving the third panel to serve as a flap over the bag. Using heather yarn, whipstitch the ends of the handle closed.

5. No closure is necessary for this bag, but you may choose to add two buttons, placing one close to the bottom of the bag, the other close to the bottom of the flap. Add a chain of about 4" to 6" (10 to 15 cm) of turquoise yarn to use as a winding closure between the two buttons. Weave in all ends.

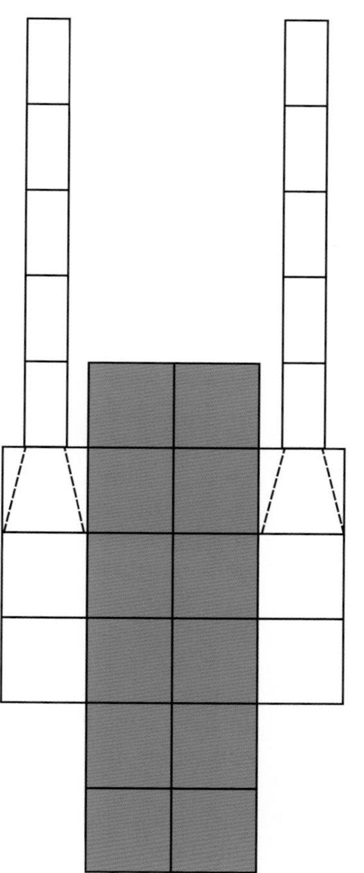

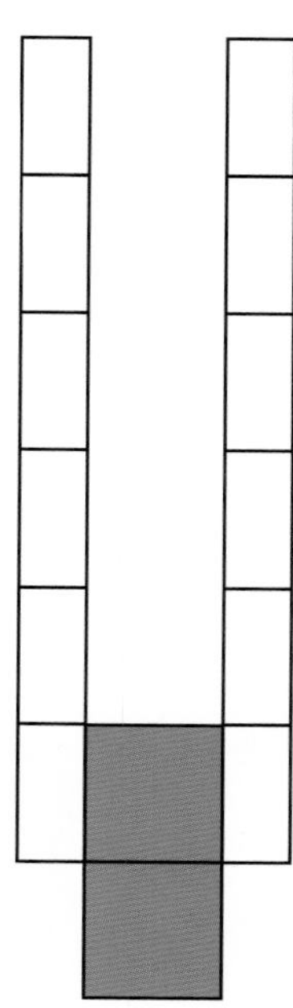

Small Monk's Bag

1. Weave:
- Two 4" x 4" squares in gold using the crossroad pattern (see page 16)
- Ten to twelve 2" x 4" weavies in teal

2. With gold yarn, single crochet around the edges of the two 4" x 4" squares and whipstitch the squares together.

3. Sew the 2" x 4" teal weavies together into a long strip using the double overcast stitch.

4. Single crochet along each side of the teal strip in gold, and single crochet across each end edge in teal.

5. Whipstitch the two long sides of the teal strip to the 4" x 4" squares. Whipstitch the bottom ends of each teal strip closed.

6. Add a button or magnetic closure if desired; see the methods suggested in the instructions for the large bag. Weave in all ends.

Caribbean Shoulder Bag

This is a shoulder bag you can carry anywhere, designed especially for the Zoom Loom. The simple design lets the qualities of your favorite yarn shine through. The bag owes much of its versatility to its construction; all of the panels have two layers so that the softer outer layer is supported by a second layer that acts as a lining and stabilizer. You can embellish the shoulder bag using Loom Blooms, originally introduced to the pin loom weaving world by Jana Trent in a 2005 article in *Spin-Off* magazine.

I've also included instructions for a variation made with a mix of 4" x 4" and 4" x 8" weavies, with additional support provided by a middle layer of quilt batting.

Finished Measurements

12" x 8" x 4" (30 x 20 x 10 cm)

Tools

- 4" x 4" pin loom
- Size G-6 (4.0 mm) crochet hook
- Tapestry needle

Yarn

- 200 yd. (183 m) variegated blue bulky (weight category 5) yarn
- 150 yd. (137 m) solid slate blue medium worsted (weight category 4) acrylic yarn
- 190 yd. (174 m) lime green medium worsted (weight category 4) acrylic yarn
- 8 yd. (7.5 m) pale blue medium worsted (weight category 4) acrylic yarn
- 8 yd. (7.5 m) pale lime medium worsted (weight category 4) acrylic yarn
- Scrap amount (less than 1 ft. [30 cm]) of complementary-color yarn for the flower

The sample shown here was made with a variegated yarn with an extremely long color repeat; when woven on a pin loom, this yarn produces an incredible variation of patternings all from the same skien. When choosing yarn for this project, look for a tweed pattern, hopefully with extended variations in color.

Notions

- 3½" x 11" (9 x 28 cm) piece of stiff plastic or cardboard to stiffen bottom of bag

Instructions

1. Weave on the 4" x 4" loom
   - Twenty squares in the variegated color
   - Seventeen squares in the complementary color
   - Twenty-five squares in the lining color
2. Stack one variegated square on top of a lining square with loops all lined up. Attach the squares together by single crocheting all the way around the edges. Repeat seventeen more times.

If you don't have a 2" x 6" loom, you can substitute ten 2" x 4" weavies (or twenty 2" x 2" squares) for the seven 2" x 6" ones.

3. Stack one complementary-color square on top of a lining square with loops all lined up. Attach the squares together by single crocheting all the way around the edges. Repeat three more times.
4. To construct the bottom of the bag, join three blue squares together in a strip using mattress stitch. Join three lime green squares together the same way. Sandwich the piece of plastic or cardboard between the blue strip and the green strip and single crochet all the way around the edge. Add an additional row of single crochet to each of the short ends in order to keep the measurements equal to those of the body of the bag.
5. Lay out the sandwiched squares as shown in the diagram and whipstitch them together. Fold the sides up and whipstitch the sides together.
6. Place the two extra variegated squares on the front of the bag for pockets. Sew or slip stitch in place.
7. With the variegated yarn, single crochet around the front flap and around the front of the bag opening. If the fabric is dimpled in at any joints between the blocks, use a half double crochet instead of a single crochet in that spot to fill it in.
8. With the solid blue yarn, join the remaining blue squares into a strip using the double overcast stitch. Fold the strap in half lengthwise and, beginning about 3" (7.5 cm) from the end, single crochet the two sides of the strap together, forming a 2" (5 cm) tube. Stop joining the edges about 3" (7.5 cm) from the other end but continue to crochet around the edge of the piece, so your edging goes all the way around the end of the strip and back up to where the join starts. Edge the other end of the strip with single crochet in the same way. Turn the strap inside out so that the crochet join is on the inside and lightly block with a stream iron and pressing cloth.
9. Using the variegated yarn, slip stitch two lines along the top of the strap. This will make the strap stronger and flatter as well as carrying the design of the bag over onto the strap. Whipstitch each crocheted end of the strap to the side of the bag with solid blue yarn, completing a circle of the solid color around the bag through the sides, bottom, and strap.

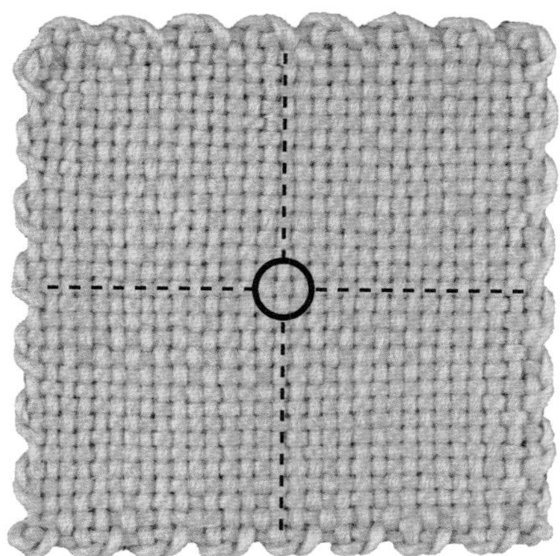

10. To make the Loom Bloom, weave one 4" x 4" weavie in pale blue and one in pale lime. Find one horizontal thread in the middle of each square and use a crochet hook to pull the thread in order to gather the fabric. Repeat the process with a vertical thread to form four petals. Knot the two pulled threads together. Use the pulled threads to seat one "bloom" inside the other. Use the contrasting yarn to add details. Sew the Loom Bloom onto the flap of the bag. Weave in all ends.

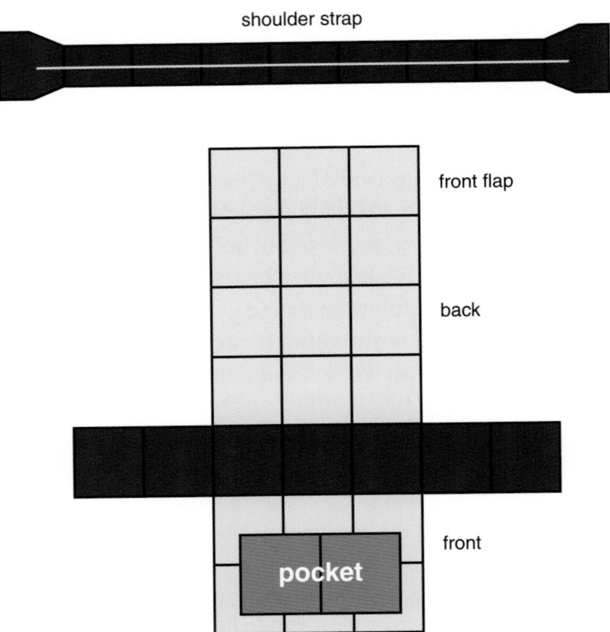

Variation

Tools

- 4" x 4" pin loom
- 4" x 8" pin loom
- 2" x 6" pin loom
- Size G-6 (4.0 mm) crochet hook
- Tapestry needle

Yarn

Medium worsted (weight category 4) acrylic, wool, or acrylic-wool blend yarn

- 200 yd. (183 m) heather rose
- 150 yd. (137 m) burgundy
- 190 yd. (174 m) pale pink
- 7.5 yd. (7 m) pale blue
- 7.5 yd. (7 m) medium blue
- 2 yd. (1.8 m) contrasting color for the flower center

Notions

- 3½" x 11" (9 x 28 cm) piece of stiff plastic or cardboard to stiffen bottom of bag
- 3 sq. ft. (0.3 m^2) of quilt batting (optional)

Instructions

1. Weave:
   - Eight 4" x 8" weavies in heather rose
   - Six 4" x 4" weavies in heather rose
   - Three 4" x 8" weavies in burgundy
   - Three 4" x 4" weavies in burgundy
   - Seven 2" x 6" weavies in burgundy
   - Ten 4" x 8" weavies in pink
   - Five 4" x 4" weavies in pink
2. Sandwich seven of the 4" x 8" heather rose weavies with pale pink weavies of the same size. If using the quilt batting, add a 3.5" x 7.75" (9 x 20 cm) piece of batting in the middle of each sandwich. Single crochet around the outside of each sandwich with heather rose yarn.
3. Sandwich four of the 4" x 4" heather rose weavies with pale pink weavies of the same size. Add a 3.5" x 3.5" (9 x 9 cm) panel of quilt batting (if using) between each pair. Single crochet around the outside of each sandwich with heather rose yarn.
4. To construct the bottom of the bag, join one 4" x 8" burgundy weavie with a 4" x 4" burgundy weavie using mattress stitch. Join a pink 4" x 8" with a pink 4" x 4" in the same way. Sandwich the 3.5" x 11" (9 x 28 cm) piece of cardboard or plastic plus a piece of batting the same size (if using) between the burgundy piece and the pink piece. Single crochet the pieces together around the whole edge. Add an additional row of single crochet to one of the short ends of the bottom in order to match the measurements of the body of the bag.
5. Lay out the lined weavies as shown in the diagram and whipstitch them together. Draw the sides up and whipstitch the sides together.
6. Attach a 4" x 8" heather rose weavie to the front of the bag for a pocket using slip stitch or blanket stitch. Add a line of stitching up the middle of the pocket to divide it into two 4" x 4" pockets.
7. Join the 2" x 6" weavies (or the substitute sizes) into a strip for the shoulder strap using the double overcast stitch.
8. Take a 4" x 4" burgundy weavie, fold it in half on the diagonal, and tuck in the corners on the folded edge to create a blunted triangle. Repeat with second 4" x 4" burgundy weavie. Stitch the point of each triangle to one end of the shoulder strap, then attach it to the bag along the diagonal fold with whipstitch.
9. To make the Loom Bloom, weave one 4" x 4" weavie in pale blue, one 4" x 4" weavie in medium blue, and one 2" x 2" weavie in hot pink. Find one horizontal thread in the middle of each square and use a crochet hook to pull the thread in order to gather the fabric. Repeat the process with a vertical thread to form four petals. Knot the two pulled threads together. Use the pulled threads to seat the three "blooms" inside each other, with the smallest on top. Add stitching for flower details. Sew the flower to the bag. Weave in all ends.

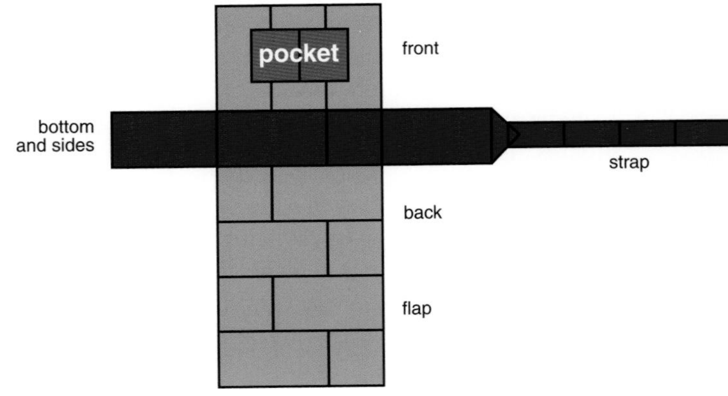

Regency-Style Reticule

If you have ever seen a movie based on a Jane Austen book, you may have noticed that the ladies carried small bags, often with drawstring loops for their wrists. This was know as a reticule. Up until the Regency Era, woman had nice big pockets underneath their dresses to carry the essentials. When fashion suddenly changed to slim muslin dresses, this exquisite little purse was born.

These reticule bags are woven in a lacy, sparkly yarn with a pattern of stars on each of their three sides, which gives them an unexpected depth. They are just big enough to hold the essentials and feature a drawstring as well as a wrist loop. Consider making one in black or colored crochet thread as well. These bags are shown unlined but could easily be lined.

Finished Measurements

4" x 4" x 6" (10 x 10 x 15 cm)

Tools

- 4" x 6" pin loom
- Size G-6 (4.0 mm) crochet hook
- Tapestry needle

Yarn

- 18 yd. (16 m) fine (weight category 2) sparkly acrylic and metallic polyester blend yarn (sample made with Lion Brand Vanna's Glamour)

Notions

- 2 yd. (1.8 m) ¼" (0.5 cm) black ribbon
- Silver beads, ¼" (8 mm) in diameter

Instructions

1. Weave three 4" x 6" weavies in the six-star pattern (see page 18).

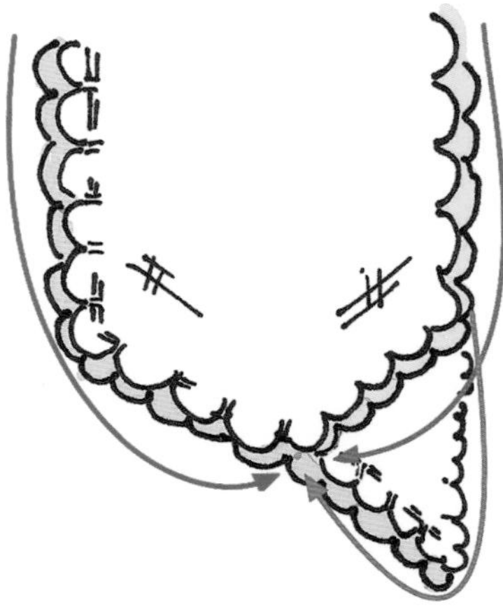

2. Join the three panels together into a three-sided piece with single crochet.
3. Work one row of double crochet around the top edge of the bag. Next, work a row in the following pattern: Half double crochet, chain 4, skip next stitch; repeat around the edge of the bag.
4. Take a 24" (60 cm) length of black ribbon, fold in two, and weave the doubled ribbon through the half double crochet row, going through every other space, to make the drawstring. Thread some silver beads onto the ribbon and knot the ends together.
5. Make a 12" (30 cm) chain with the remainder of the black ribbon. Tie the ends of the chain together and sew to the inside of the back edge of the bag to make the wrist loop. Weave in all ends.

Variation

Use several strands of yarn for the drawstring tie, and make a chain with two strands of yarn held together for a matching wrist loop.

Water Bottle Holder

Many of the items I make are at the suggestion of family members. I had several people request a pattern for a water bottle holder but I felt constrained by the fact that everything that is produced on a pin loom is square or rectangular. How could I make a round carrier with square pieces? It was only in making my little stuffed cacti (see page 67) that I realized how gracefully three squares can turn into one column. I followed the same approach here. The water bottle is three strips of weavies that come together to make a round holder with a triangular base. This size is perfect for the common 20 to 24 oz. water bottle.

The water bottle holder can be made with less than one 100-yd. skein of yarn. Since you are carrying it with you—or making it for someone you really care about—consider splurging on a spectacular yarn.

Finished Measurements

5" x 10" (12.5 x 25 cm)

Tools

- 4" x 4" pin loom
- Size G-6 (4.0 mm) crochet hook
- Tapestry needle

Yarn

Bulky (weight category 5) yarn (sample made with Sensations It's A Wrap in blue-turquoise)
- 72 yd. (66 m) main color

Instructions

1. Weave nine 4" x 4" squares.

2. Join the squares into three strips of three squares each, using the double overcast stitch.

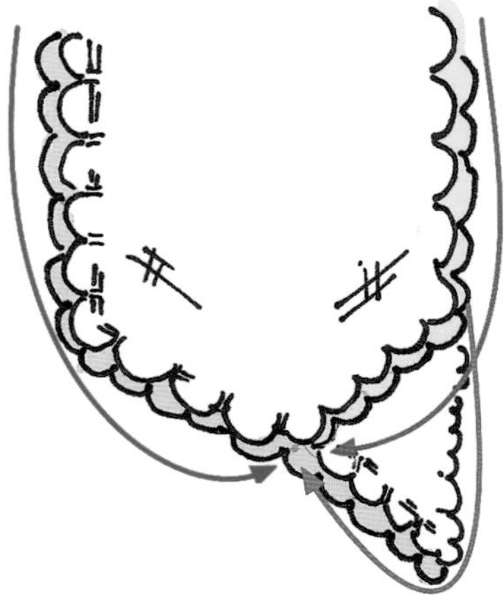

3. Join the long sides of the strips together (again, using the double overcast stitch), sewing down each side and around the bottom corner, with the three seams meeting in the middle of the base, as shown in the diagram.
4. Turn the piece so the seam ridges are on the inside.
5. With three strands of the main yarn or a solid coordinating-color yarn, make a braid approximately 48" long; knot the ends.
6. Using a tapestry needle, weave the braid through the fabric about ½" from the top edge. Knot the ends of the braid together on the inside of the holder. This carrying loop can be tightened around the top of the holder and is long enough to wear across your body. Weave in all ends.

Reversible Hobo Bag

This bag is a product of weaving too much. Sooner or later you will have extra squares piling up that do not quite fit into the planned project but they are just too nice, too lovely to be thrown aside. This design is intended for those squares. Its easy to make, looks great with random weavings and is reversible. I originally planned that the bag would feature the zigzag pattern of single crochet join running all over it. The join stands out and contrasts nicely with the weavies. However when I turned it inside out, I found out that it looks pretty great that way, too. So it's reversible: You choose the way you like it best.

Because I had a number of tan, cream, and pale yellow weavies, I decided to use them exclusively in the strap. You might prefer to maintain the same color combinations throughout the bag and strap.

Finished Measurements

Bag: 15" x 10" (38 x 25 cm)
Strap: 3" x 40" (7.5 x 100 cm)

Tools

- 4" x 4" pin loom
- Size G-6 (4.0 mm) crochet hook
- Tapestry needle

Yarn

- 43 leftover 4" x 4" squares in assorted colors and textures, or enough yarn in various colors to weave 43 squares (each square takes 7.5 yd. [7 m] of yarn, so you will need about 325 yd. [300 m] total)
- 50 yd. (46 m) yarn for joining squares

Notions

- Heavy pendant, 2" to 3" (5 to 7.5 cm) in diameter

Instructions

1. If making new squares, weave twenty-eight 4" x 4" squares for the bag and fifteen for the strap. This makes a stretchy 40" (100 cm) strap. You may want to experiment with a longer or shorter strap.
2. Lay out the squares as shown in the diagram, working to balance contrasting colors and textures. If you have variegated squares, you may want to alternate them with solid squares.
3. Join the squares together with single crochet in one or more contrasting colors. You can work the joining continuously by zigzagging back and forth across the bag. I found that I had to lay the squares back down in the original layout after each join in order not to lose my place. It would probably be possible to continue the crochet zigzag around both sides of the bag, but I suggest joining the squares on one side, then joining the squares on the other, and finally joining both sides of the bag.
4. Fold down the four squares at the top edge and stitch to the inside. Weave in and trim all ends.

5. Lay out the squares for the strap in an overlapping pattern, as shown in the diagram. I suggest basting them together with a running stitch straight down the center of the strip first to hold them in place temporarily. Fold the corners of each square over in order to form a 3" strap. Single crochet along both edges of the strap. Take some stitches through the corners of the squares where they come together for reinforcement. Lightly block the strap.
6. You will notice that the front and back corner squares of your bag (light green in the diagrams) can overlap. Place one end of the strap between two overlapping corner squares and sew this sandwich of three layers of weavies together. You can go over the stitching with slip stitch in order to carry on the crochet design, but I suggest stitching first. Repeat on the other side.
7. Take two strands of any complementary-color yarn and chain approximately 12" (30 cm). Thread on the pendant and attach the ends of the chain to the top back side of the bag. The weight of the pendant will help keep the bag closed and will work whether the bag is inside out or right side out (you decide which side will be the right side and which the inside). Weave in all ends.

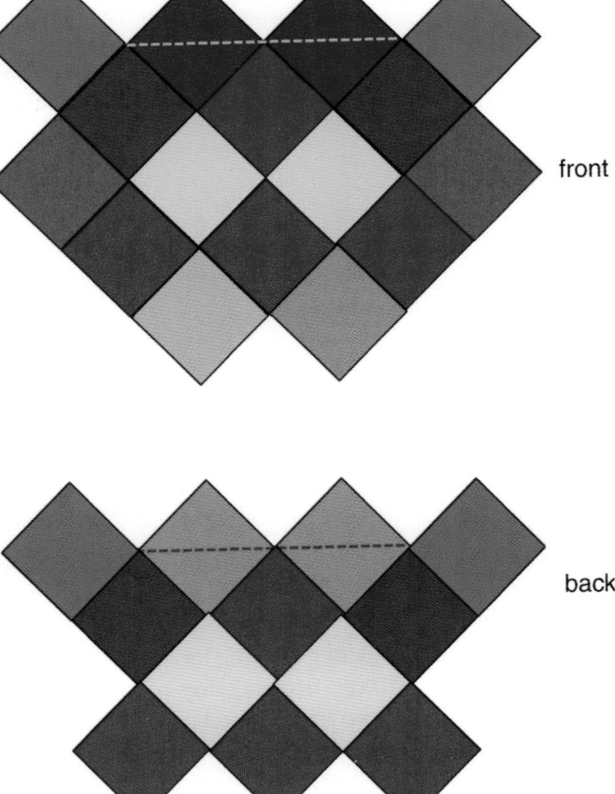

CHAPTER THREE

Gifts and Home Décor

Holiday Banners

These two little banners were the work of an afternoon and evening spent with good friends. The alphabet was simple and quick and the pumpkin embellishment came from a craft store. These banners are easy to make and easy to personalize with your own special holiday message.

Finished Measurements

BOO: 4" x 16" (10 x 40 cm)
NOEL: 24" x 4" (60 x 10 cm)

Tools

- 4" x 4" pin loom
- Tapestry needle

Yarn

BOO

Medium worsted (weight category 4) cotton yarn (sample made with Lily Sugar 'n Cream)

- 20 yd. (18 m) white
- 20 yd. (18 m) orange

NOEL

Medium worsted (weight category 4) acrylic yarn

- 24 yd. (22 m) red
- 24 yd. (22 m) green
- 2 yd. (1.8 m) white

Notions

BOO

- 5" (12.5 cm) wooden dowel, ¼" (6 mm) in diameter
- Jack-o'-lantern embellishment

NOEL

- Approximately 1 yd. (0.9 m) red ribbon, ¼" (6 mm) wide

CROSS-STITCHING ON PIN LOOM FABRIC

One of the several advantages of pin loom weaving is that it produces a lovely, even weave. If you have any experience with cross-stitch, it will likely cross your mind that this would be great fabric for cross-stitching. If you don't have any experience with cross-stitch, this fabric is a good place to start, because the stitches will be large and the medium is well suited to simple patterns. For this project, each cross-stitch should cover a square of four threads.

If you are interested in further exploring the use of cross-stitch on weavies, do check out the many vintage Weave-It pattern books available at Eloomanation.com. There are a number of adult and baby blankets in them that include cross-stitch patterns.

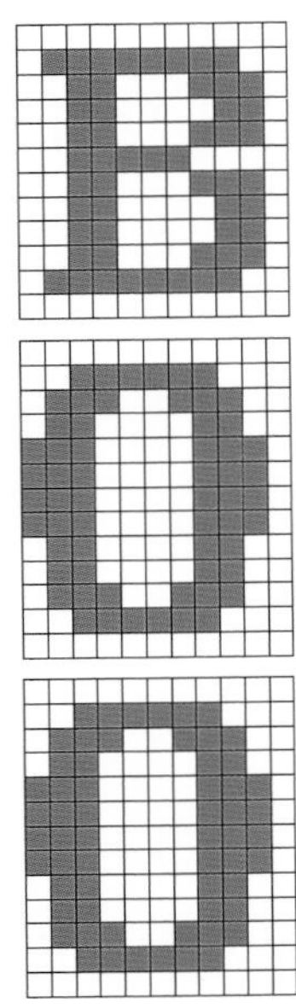

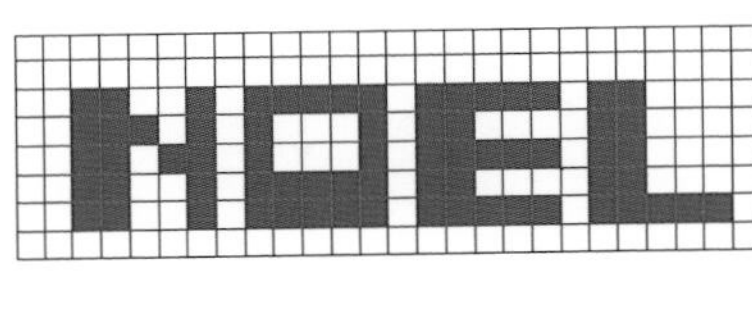

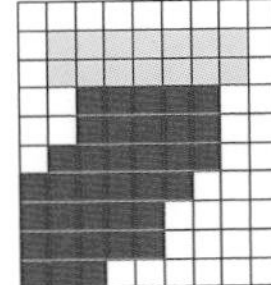

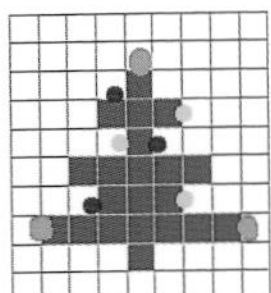

Instructions

1. Weave:

   for BOO:
   - Two orange squares
   - Two white squares

   for NOEL:
   - Three green squares
   - Three red squares
2. Add the cross-stitch letters, following the patterns on this page.
3. Join the squares using the mattress stitch.
4. Finishing:

   BOO: Add Halloween embellishments or stitch additional motifs such as pumpkin or ghost at the bottom of the banner. Attach the top edge of the banner to a wooden dowel or other support with a loose overcast stitch and white crochet thread.

   NOEL: Weave red ribbon through every third set of top loops, leaving enough ribbon on either end to hang the banner.

Baby Name Banner

This is a great way to welcome home a new baby. Use an alphabet font that appeals to you, either from the extensive resources available online or from your own collection. Keep in mind that the 6" x 6" weavie gives you a 48-by-48 grid and the 4" x 4" weavie gives you a 32-by-32 grid. The example shown here was made in colors to match the Sweetheart Baby Blanket.

Tools

- 4" x 4" pin loom or 6" x 6" pin loom
- Tapestry needle

Yarn

Medium worsted (weight category 4) yarn (sample made with Vanna's Choice Baby Yarn)

- 16.25 yd. (14.9 m) for each 6" x 6" weavie or 7.5 yd. (6.9 m) for each 4" x 4" weavie
- Scrap amounts of contrasting yarn for cross-stitching

Notions

- 3 to 6 ft. (1 to 2 m) of light cord or ribbon to hang the banner

Instructions

1. Weave the number of squares needed to spell out the baby's name.
2. Count from the center of each square to establish your starting place for each letter.
3. Cross-stitch the letters in your choice of contrasting color yarn.
4. Use a tapestry needle to weave the cord or ribbon through the loops along the top edges of the banner squares, leaving several feet of cord at each end of the banner. To keep the squares from bunching up, knot the cord at the beginning and end of each square.

Old-Fashioned Dishcloths

Who knew that making a really good dishcloth could be so simple and fun? Weaving a dishcloth is quicker than the normal weaving because you use a very open pattern to give the cloth lots of bumpy surfaces. These dishcloths work great in the kitchen, and they make a wonderful last-minute hostess or housewarming gift when wrapped around a bar of artisanal soap. And you get to modestly admit that you made them yourself!

You are making a panel of four 4" x 4" squares. Keep in mind that you can always choose to make larger dishcloths by making larger panels or making them from larger squares. I find that the dishcloth made of four squares works very well, where a larger square made up of nine squares becomes a little too bulky.

Finished Measurements

8" x 8" (20 x 20 cm)

Tools

- 4" x 4" pin loom
- Size G-6 (4.0 mm) crochet hook

Yarn

- 45 yd. (41 m) medium worsted (weight category 4) cotton yarn

Sample made in Lily Sugar 'n Cream

Instructions

1. Weave four 4" x 4" weavies using the eight-rib pattern. If you want to make stripes, wind the first color on for the first two layers, then tie on the second color and wind on the last layer and weave with the second color.

2. Use the single crochet join to attatch the squares together in pairs, then join the pairs together with the rib patterns perpendicular to each other, as shown in the diagram. The single crochet will leave a ridge across the piece, which will make a more effective dishcloth.
3. Edge the dishcloth with half double crochet. Weave in all ends.

Two Pictorial Wall Hangings

These mini afghans let you make a beautiful finished piece on an easy, "doable" scale. Try these patterns, then branch out and add a few scenes from your own neighborhood. These pieces make great wall hangings, or you can use them as pillow tops or join several together for an album quilt.

Finished Measurements

Approximately 20" x 16" (50 x 40 cm)

House and Lighthouse

Tools

- 2" x 2" pin loom
- 4" x 4" pin loom
- 2" x 4" pin loom
- Size G-6 (4.0 mm) crochet hook
- Tapestry needle

Yarn

Medium worsted (weight category 4) acrylic yarn

- 50 yd. (46 m) pale blue
- 36 yd. (33 m) variegated sky blue
- 20 yd. (18 m) brick red
- 8 yd. (7.3 m) true red
- 12 yd. (11 m) off-white
- 38 yd. (35 m) tan
- 4 yd. (3.7 m) variegated green-blue
- 4 yd. (3.7 m) gray blue
- 20 yd. (18 m) gray tweed
- 2 yd. (1.8 m) yellow
- 20 yd. (18 m) charcoal
- 4.5 yd. (4.1 m) medium brown
- Scrap amount (less than 1 yd. [0.9 m]) each of yellow-orange, medium blue, and dark brown

When weaving directions call for two yarns in the weave, wind the first two layers in the first color of yarn, then wind the third layer and weave with second color.

Instructions

1. Weave (in plain weave unless otherwise specified):
   - Six 4" x 4" weavies in pale blue and variegated sky blue
   - Five 2" x 4" weavies in pale blue and variegated sky blue
   - Two 2" x 2" weavies in pale blue and variegated sky blue
   - One 2" x 2" weavie in pale blue
   - One 2" x 4" weavie in pale blue
   - Two 2" x 4" weavies in gray blue and variegated green-blue
   - Five 4" x 4" weavies in tan
   - One 2" x 4" weavie in medium brown
   - Three 2" x 4" weavies in charcoal
   - One 2" x 2" weavie in yellow
   - Five 2" x 4" weavies in gray tweed
   - Two 4" x 4" weavies in brick red
   - One 2" x 4" weavie in off-white and brick red, using the eight-rib pattern (see page 16)

   For the three following weavies (which make up the lighthouse), substitute charcoal for the main color on the first four passes through, then use the main color for one pass, then charcoal for two, then the main color for one, then charcoal for one; complete the weavie from this point on in the main color. The idea is to create an appearance of shadow on one side of the lighthouse.
   - One 2" x 4" weavie in off-white with shading
   - One 4" x 4" weavie in off-white with shading
   - One 4" x 4" weavie in true red with shading
2. Lay one brick red 4" x 4" square on top of a tan 4" x 4" square. Sew the squares together on the diagonal. Open the piece so that the two red triangles are now on top of each other and the two tan triangles are on top of each other. This square represents part of the house gable.
3. Lay one brick red 4" x 4" square on top of a sky blue 4" x 4" square. Sew them together on the diagonal. Open the piece as before so that you have two red triangles on one side and two sky blue triangles on the other. This square is the other half of the house gable.
4. Lay out the weavies as shown in the diagram (leave the flag, lighthouse flame, lighthouse roof, and house's windows, door, and porch roof aside to be appliquéd on later). Use the mattress stitch to join like colors. When joining unlike colors, use the double overcast stitch. Make sure the shadows are lined up in the blocks for the lighthouse.
5. Single crochet around the edge of the piece using charcoal at the bottom and lower sides and pale blue around the sky area.
6. Place the yellow square at the top of the lighthouse and sew it in place with whipstitch in yellow yarn. Turn under the corners of a charcoal 2" x 4" weavie to represent the lighthouse roof and sew it in place with charcoal yarn. Embroider the light on the yellow square with yellow-orange.
7. Put the flag in place, and sew it down in off-white. Use satin stitch to cover up the red in the upper left corner of the flag with medium blue, leaving some traces of white visible for stars. Add two rows of slip stitch in medium brown for the flagpole, then add a line of running stitch in dark brown to one side for shading.
8. Turn the edges of the 2" x 2" and 2" x 4" weavies under get pieces that are the right size and shape for windows; sew in place. Use the brown 2" x 4" weavie for the door. Embroider the door frame and windows in satin stitch, using dark brown for the door frame and off-white for the windows.
9. Use mattress stitch to sew the two charcoal 2" x 4" weavies end to end to create the porch roof. Fold the top edge under approximately ½" (1 cm) and sew the piece in place along the sides and top. Leave the bottom edge loose for more dimension.
10. Add a line of running stitch in brown yarn along the side and top of the house roof for shading.
11. Weave in all ends. Block lightly on reverse side.

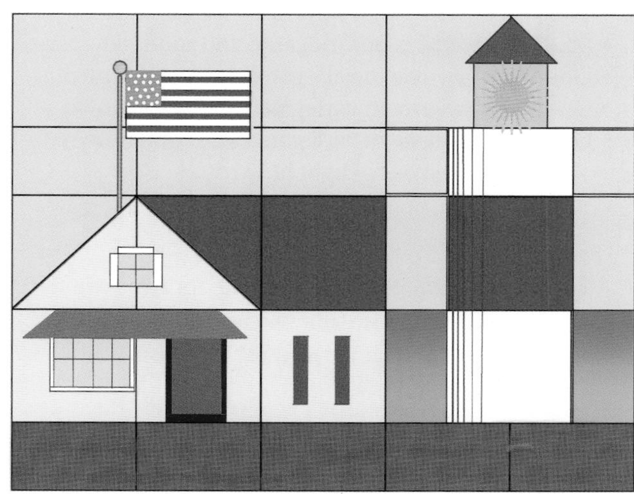

Barn and Silo

This barn and silo wall hanging portrays an old Minnesota farmstead. Old silos made from firebrick, with painted checkerboards at the top, are common features of the landscape in that part of the country.

Tools

- 2" x 2" pin loom
- 4" x 4" pin loom
- 2" x 4" pin loom
- 4" x 6" pin loom
- Size G-6 (4.0 mm) crochet hook
- Tapestry needle

Yarn

Medium worsted (weight category 4) acrylic yarn

- 23 yd. (21 m) variegated blue
- 27 yd. (25 m) light blue
- 34 yd. (31 m) variegated red
- 38 yd. (35 m) solid red
- 8 yd. (7.3 m) variegated green
- 10 yd. (9.1 m) solid green
- 11 yd. (10 m) variegated brown
- 11 yd. (10 m) solid brown
- 23 yd. (21 m) dark gray
- 8 yd. (7.3 m) light brown
- Scrap amounts (1 yd. [0.9 m] or less) of yellow, dark gray, and cream

Instructions

1. Weave:
    - Three 4" x 4" weavies in dark gray
    - Two 2" x 4" weavies in variegated and solid green
    - Five 4" x 4" weavies in variegated and solid blue
    - One 2" x 4" weavie in variegated and solid blue
    - Two 2" x 2" weavies in variegated and solid blue
    - Two 4" x 6" weavies in variegated and solid red
    - Six 4" x 4" weavies in variegated and solid red
    - One 4" x 6" weavie in variegated and solid brown
    - One 2" x 4" weavie in variegated and solid brown
    - One 2" x 2" weavie in variegated and solid brown
    - Two 2" x 4" weavies in light brown

When weaving directions call for two yarns in the weave, wind the first two layers in the first color of yarn, then wind the third layer and weave with second color.

2. Lay one red 4" x 4" square on top of a gray 4" x 4" square. Sew them together on the diagonal. Open the piece so that the two red triangles are on top of each other and the two charcoal triangles are on top of each other. This square will be the part of the gable.
3. Take a 4" x 4" red square and fold it in half diagonally. This piece will be the other half of the barn gable and will be attached to a piece of sky and a piece of the silo.
4. Lay the woven pieces out as shown in the diagram and sew them together. Use the mattress stitch when you are joining two matching pieces and double overcast stitch when you are joining different pieces and want a harder line between them (for example, between the roof and sky).
5. Single crochet around the edge of the piece, with cream around the light areas and brown around the darker areas.
6. Embroider the details on the mat. Use satin stitch to add small windows to the barn in dark gray yarn and the painted brickwork on the silo in cream. Add a line of running stitch or overcast stitch in charcoal yarn to indicate the barn doors. Slip stitch a yellow spiral in the upper right corner for the sun.
7. Use a crochet hook to gently pull the up approximately ⅛" loops of the brown variegated yarn through the brown fabric in the lower right corner of the piece to add texture. Cluster the loops to give the appearance of rocks sticking out of a rock foundation wall.
8. Weave in all ends. Block lightly on reverse side.

Tiny Stuffed Heart

Use this tiny stuffed heart as a charm for a necklace or bracelet. Cover your heart with tiny buttons or your choice of bling.

Finished Measurements

2" x 2" (5 x 5 cm)

Tools

- 2" x 2" pin loom
- Size G-6 (4.0 mm) crochet hook
- Tapestry needle

Yarn

Medium worsted (weight category 4) wool yarn
- 5 yd. (4.5 m) red

Notions

- Polyester fiberfill
- Buttons and/or beads for decoration

Instructions

1. Weave two 2" x 2" squares.

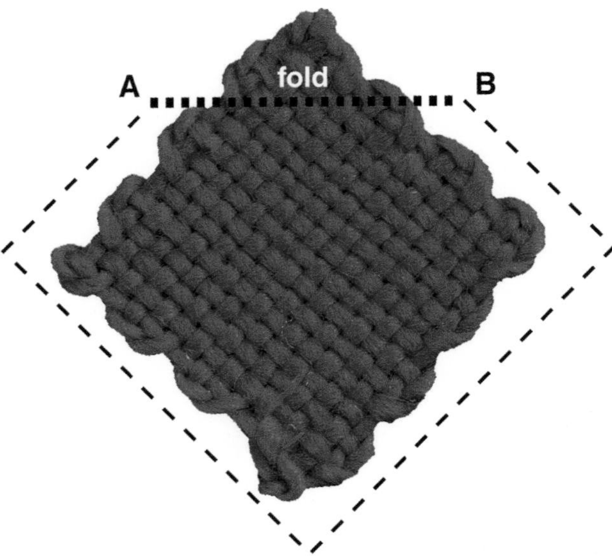

2. Stack the two squares with loops matching and single crochet approximately ¾ of the way around edges of the squares. Chain 2 at the middle corner, but do not chain at the two side corners. Fasten off securely.
3. Turn the piece inside out and fold the top (uncrocheted) corners down into the heart.
4. Stuff tightly.
5. The top of the heart will now gape open due to the stuffing. Stitch the top closed, pulling it together and down to form the dip of the heart. The tight stuffing helps pull the top edge down to form a perfect little heart.
6. Decorate your heart with tiny buttons or beads. Weave in all ends.

Soft Bowls

These colorful little bowls add a spark to the room and make great containers for jewelry, potpourri, decorative seashells . . . anything but soup! They are great for gifts as well. The construction takes less time than you might think, since the four sides of the bowl are each created from one 4" x 4" square, folded in half.

You can use a wide variety of yarns for this project. Even if the woven squares are very thin and soft, the quilt batting will provide the necessary stiffness for the bowl to keep its shape. The bright-colored bowls shown here were made with a single twist wool in high-contrast colors. The woven pattern highlights the luminosity and rich colors of the single-ply yarn.The denim-gray bowl was made with an overdyed wool in indigo tones woven with a gray heather worsted.

Finished Measurements

5" x 5" x 2½" (12.5 x 12.5 x 6 cm)

Tools

- 4" x 4" pin loom
- Size G-6 (4.0 mm) crochet hook
- Tapestry needle

Yarn

Medium worsted (weight category 4) single-ply acrylic-wool blend yarn

Bright Pink and Blue Bowls

- 50 yd. (46 m) yarn in main color
- 14 yd. (13 m) yarn in contrasting color
- 4 yd. (3.7 m) yarn for contrasting crochet edge

Denim-Gray Bowl

Medium worsted (weight category 4) wool yarn

- 45 yd. (41 m) variegated indigo
- 46 yd. (42 m) gray heather

Notions

- ⅔ to 1 sq. ft. (0.06 to 0.1 m^2) quilt batting

TIP: The more layers of batting you use, the stiffer and puffier the bowl will be. If you don't have any batting lying around, you can substitute with felt made from an old sweater or any fabric scraps.

Instructions

Bright Pink and Blue Bowls

1. Weave:
    - Five 4" x 4" squares in the main color
    - One 4" x 4" square in the contrasting color
2. Fold a main color square in half and insert two or three layers of quilt batting inside. Single crochet around all four edges with the main color. Repeat with three more squares.
3. Sandwich two or three layers of quilt batting between the remaining two squares. Using the main color, single crochet around the piece (with the main color side up).
4. Whipstitch the sides of the box to the bottom, then whipstitch the sides to each other.
5. Finish by crocheting around the top edge of the box.
   Option 1 (Blue Bowl): Work 1 row of single crochet in pink, then 1 row of single crochet in red.
   Option 2 (Pink Bowl): Work 1 row of half double crochet in red, then 1 row of single crochet in blue. Roll the blue edge in and whipstitch to the inside of the bowl.
6. Weave in all ends.

Denim-Gray Bowl

1. Weave eight 4" x 4" squares, using the variegated indigo to wrap the first two layers; use gray heather to wrap the third layer and weave the fourth layer.
2. Fold a square in half and insert two or three layers of quilt batting inside. Single crochet around all four edges with the main color. Repeat with three more squares.
3. Sandwich two or three layers of quilt batting between two more squares. Single crochet around the piece.
4. Whipstitch the sides of the box to the bottom, then whipstitch the sides to each other.
5. Work 1 row of half double crochet around the top edge of the bowl in indigo. Next work 1 row of single crochet in gray, then 1 row of half double crochet in indigo. Roll the crochet edge to the inside and stitch in place with gray yarn.
6. Single crochet around each of the two remaining 4" x 4" squares in gray.
7. Work 1 row of half double crochet around one of these squares in indigo.
8. Stack these two 4" x 4" squares with three layers of batting in between. Whipstitch the smaller square to the gray single crochet row on the larger square to form a lip so that the woven lid will fit neatly on the bowl. Weave in all ends on both pieces.

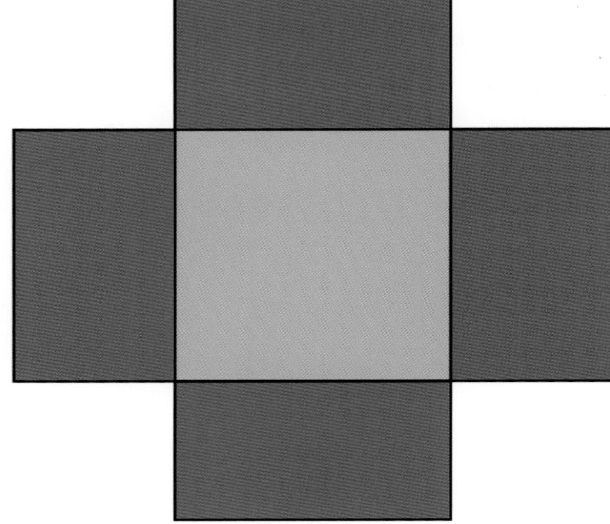

Little Bird Chain

These tiny birds can be made in a few minutes and can perch anywhere you like.

Finished Measurements

2½" x 1" (6.4 x 2.5 cm)

Tools

- 2" x 2" pin loom
- Size G-6 (4.0 mm) crochet hook
- Tapestry needle

Yarn

Light worsted (weight category 3) wool or acrylic yarn
- 3 yd. (2.7 m) per bird

Notions

- Very small amount of stuffing

Instructions

1. Weave a 2" x 2" square.

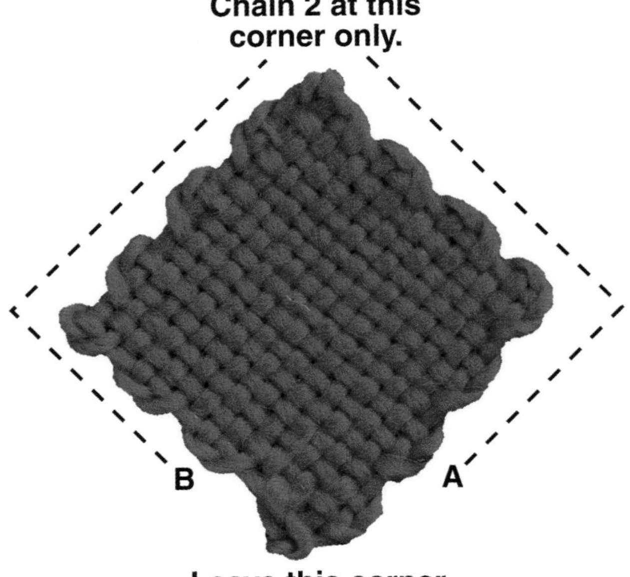

Leave this corner uncrocheted to form the bird tail.

2. Work sc around the edge of the square from from point A to point B (see diagram); do not chain at the side corners, but chain 2 at the top corner.
3. Fold the weavie diagonally so that the two crochet sides match up.
4. Whipstitch the crochet edge, starting from the middle corner. Leave an opening at the tail end.
5. Stuff the bird, then stitch it closed, leaving the corner fanned out to represent the bird's tail. Weave in all ends.

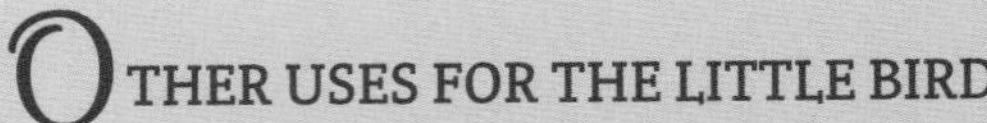

Perching Bird: Run a short loop of floral wire or dark wrapped wire through the bird's belly to perch it wherever you choose.

Bird Mobile: Make a number of birds and string each one on a piece of yarn. Attach the yarn to several bamboo skewers to make a mobile.

Bird Ornaments: Attach a loop of matching or contrasting yarn to the top of the Little Bird to make a Christmas tree ornament.

Finishing the Bird Chain

Weave a selection of birds in your favorite colors. Run a length of yarn through the birds, knotting after each bird so that they do not slide together.

Cactus in Bloom

For many people, these cacti fall in the "small, lovable gifts" category. I classify them as "plants that don't die in my house." I first made some woven cacti when I was tasked with providing table favors for a Mexican-themed dinner. They went over really well. If you find yourself in need of a quick decoration or hostess gift, keep these in mind. The cactus also provides a wonderful vehicle to exhibit Jana Trent's Loom Blooms.

Finished Measurements

Approximately 4" x 6" (10 x 15 cm)

Tools

- 4" x 4" pin loom
- 2" x 2" pin loom
- 2" x 4" pin loom
- Size G-6 (4.0 mm) crochet hook
- Tapestry needle

Yarn

Variation 1

- 12 yd. (11 m) dusty green medium worsted (weight category 4) wool-acrylic blend yarn
- 14 yd. (13 m) gray heather medium worsted (weight category 4) wool-acrylic blend yarn
- Scrap amount of gray or gold super fine (weight category 1) yarn (for cactus needles)
- 9.5 yd. (8.7 m) yellow-gold medium worsted (weight category 4) wool-acrylic blend yarn

Variation 2

Medium worsted (weight category 4) wool yarn
- 18 yd. (16 m) speckled or tweedy light green
- 7 yd. (6 m) solid green
- 6 yd. (5 m) yellow

Notions

- Modeling clay or Play-Doh
- Miniature flower pot, small basket, or other container with an opening about 3" to 4" (7.5 to 10 cm) wide

Instructions

Variation 1

1. Weave:
   - Three 4" x 4" weavies, winding first two layers in green and winding third layer and weaving in gray
   - One 4" x 4" weavie in gold
   - One 2" x 2" weavie in gold

2. Using green yarn and single crochet, join the three green and gray weavies in a three-sided shape. Taking one side at a time, crochet from bottom of cactus to the middle of the top, leaving long ends; after you have completed the three side joins, come back to the top and knot the ends together.
3. Stuff the cactus, then stitch a running thread around the bottom edge and pull it closed. Tie off but leave the threads long, as you can use them to secure the cactus to the base.
4. Using the gray yarn, stitch a vertical line down the middle of each 4" x 4" square, then pull the shape in to form a suggestion of separate columns.
5. Add needles by pulling short lengths of soft yarn through the cactus and trimming off on both sides.

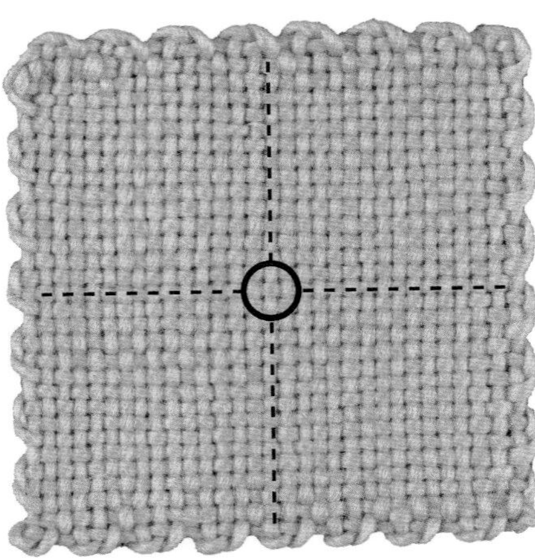

6. Find a horizontal thread in the middle of each gold square. Using a crochet hook, pull the thread to gather the fabric. Repeat the process with a vertical thread to form four petals. Knot the pulled threads together.
7. Add the flowers to the top of the cactus, with the smaller one seated inside the larger. Finish with a few green French knots for stamens. Weave in all ends.
8. Seat the cactus on a lump of clay or Play-Doh for weight and to obtain the proper height within your container. Secure the plant to the base by wrapping the hanging threads left in step 3 around the base. Place the cactus in its container.

Variation 2

1. Weave:
   - Three 2" x 4" weavies in green tweed
   - Three 2" x 2" weavies in green tweed
   - Three 2" x 2" weavies in yellow
2. Using solid green and single crochet, joing the three green 2" x 2" weavies into a short three-sided cactus column; in the same way, make a taller three-sided cactus column using the three 2" x 4" weavies. After joining the sides, knots the ends left at the top of each cactus together to close the top. Stitch the two colums together at the base with two flat sides together.
3. Stuff the cacti from the bottom and stitch the bottoms closed.
4. Find one horizontal thread in the middle of each yellow square. Using a crochet hook, pull the thread to gather the fabric. Repeat the process with a vertical thread to form four petals. Knot the two pulled threads together.
5. Attach two of the flowers to the top of the larger cactus and add French knots in green for stamens. Pinch the other flower so that it appears half closed, wrap a few turns of solid green yarn around the bottom, and sew it to the other cactus. Weave in all ends.
6. Seat the cacti on clay or Play-Doh for weight and to obtain the proper height within your container. Secure the plant to the base by wrapping the hanging threads left in step 3 around the base. Place the cactus in its container.

Ducks and Duckling

These mallard ducks are both sturdy and cuddly. They make good kids' toys, but you could probably sneak them in as a Dad's Day gift if he's into hunting. The big surprise in making the ducks is what a terrific duck beak you can make with a 2" x 2" square weavie.

Finished Measurements

Duck: 6.5" x 5" (16.5 x 12.7 cm)
Duckling: 5" x 5" (12.7 x 12.7 cm)

Tools

- 2" x 2" pin loom
- 4" x 4" pin loom
- 2" x 4" pin loom
- 4" x 6" pin loom
- Size G-6 (4.0 mm) crochet hook
- Tapestry needle

Yarn

Medium worsted (weight category 4) acrylic yarn

Male Duck

- 45 yd. (41 m) medium brown
- 8 yd. (7.3 m) light brown
- 2 yd. (1.8 m) gold
- 8 yd. (7.3 m) teal
- 2 yd. (1.8 m) cream
- 1 yd. (0.9 m) dark brown

Female Duck

- 25 yd. (23 m) medium brown
- 12 yd. (11 m) light brown
- 7 yd. (6.4 m) gold
- 1 yd. (0.9 m) teal
- 3 yd. (2.7 m) cream

Duckling

- 23 yd. (21 m) pale yellow
- 2 yd. (1.8 m) gold
- Scrap amount (less than 1 yd. [0.9 m]) dark brown

Notions

- Polyester fiberfill
- Plastic pellets or small beans

Instructions

Ducks

1. For a male duck, weave:
   - Two 2" x 2" weavies in teal (head)
   - Two 4" x 6" weavies in medium brown and light brown—wind with medium brown; weave with light brown (body)
   - Two 4" x 4" weavies in medium brown (wings)
   - One 2" x 4" weavie in medium brown and light brown—wind with medium brown; weave with light brown (base)
   - One 2" x 2" weavie in gold (beak)
   - One 2" x 2" weavie in teal and medium brown—wind the first two layers with teal, then wind the third layer and weave with medium brown (tail)

   For a female duck, weave:
   - Two 2" x 2" weavies in gold (head)
   - Two 4" x 6" weavies in light brown and medium brown—wind with light brown; weave with medium brown (body)
   - Two 4" x 4" weavies in medium brown (wings)
   - One 2" x 4" weavie in light brown and medium brown—wind with light brown; weave with medium brown (base)
   - One 2" x 2" weavie in light brown (beak)
   - One 2" x 2" weavie in medium brown and light brown—wind with medium brown; weave with light brown (tail)
2. Single crochet around the edge of each of the 2" x 2" weavies for head, rounding out the top two corners by turning them in slightly and not chaining at these corners (chain 2 at the bottom two corners as usual.) Whipstitch the squares together in same color, leaving the bottom open, as shown in the diagram.
3. Double crochet around bottom of head in cream. Stuff the head and neck.

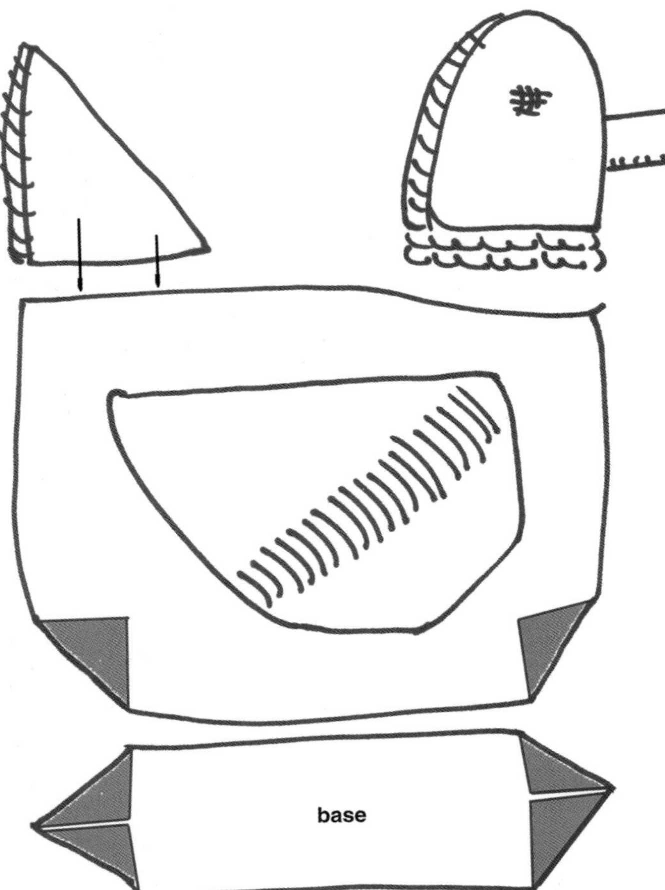

4. Turn under three of the corners of each 4" x 6" weavie and single crochet around the edge in the dominant color, going through the fabric along the folded-in edges. The one unturned corner will form the tail.
5. Turn in all four corners of the 2" x 4" base, and single crochet around the edge in the dominant color.
6. Whipstitch the two sides of the body to the base. Bring the sides of the body together and whipstitch the sides, then bring the top edges of these pieces together and whipstitch along the top, leaving a 2" (5 cm) opening for the head. Add plastic pellets in the bottom of the body for stability, then stuff the rest of the body.
7. Place the head and neck onto the opening, adding more stuffing as needed, and sew into place with the same color used on the body.

8. Single crochet around the edge of the tail, then fold the piece in half diagonally and sew along one side of the triangle formed. Add a little stuffing and place over the tail end of the duck. Sew in place in the body color.

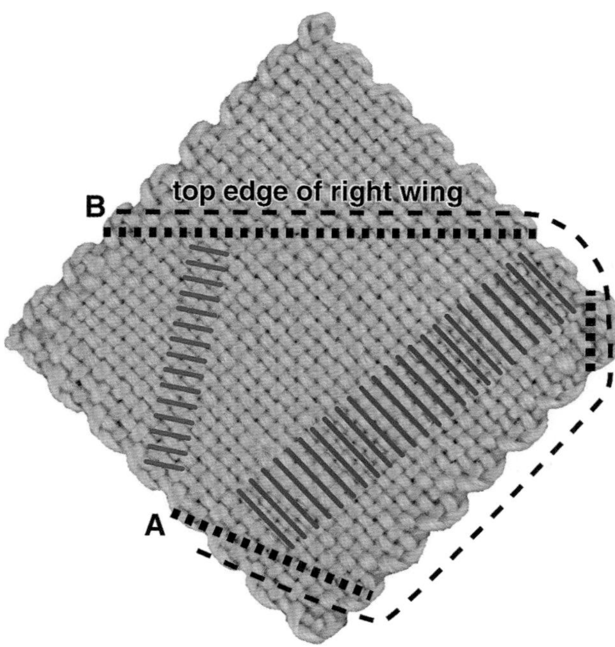

9. Turn under the corners of the two 4" x 4" weavies for the wings, as shown in the diagram. Single crochet around the edge from A to B in dark brown. Sew the wings to the body using the dominant body color. You can sew all the way around or leave the top of the wing open (making a great little pocket on each side of the duck).

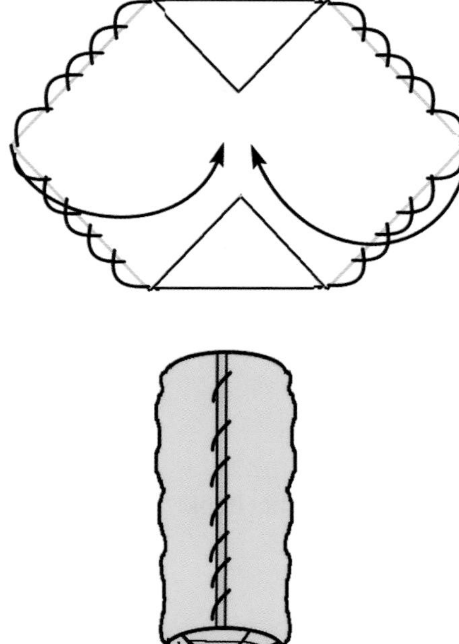

10. Fold in two corners of the 2" x 2" square for the beak to create a piece 1¼" (3 cm) across. Fold in the other two corners and roll the piece up into a tight tube. Sew this tube closed at the end and along the length. Attach the open end to the head with the beak color.
11. Embroider eyes on the head in a contrasting color. Weave in all ends.

Duckling

1. Weave:
   - Two 2" x 2" weavies in pale yellow
   - Three 2" x 4" weavies in pale yellow
   - One 2" x 2" weavie in gold
2. Single crochet around the edge of each of the pale yellow 2" x 2" weavies, rounding out the top two corners by turning them in slightly and not chaining at these corners (chain 2 at bottom two corners as usual). Whipstitch the pieces together in same color, leaving the bottom open, as shown in the diagram below. Stuff the head.

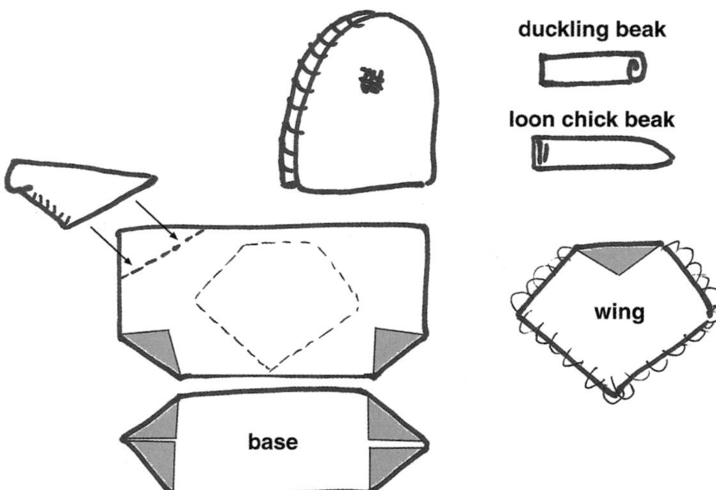

3. Turn in the two bottom corners of two of the 2" x 4" weavies (the sides) and single crochet around the edge in same color.
4. Turn in all four corners of the remaining 2" x 4" weavie (the base) as shown in the diagram and single crochet around the edge.
5. Whipstitch the two sides to the base, then whipstitch the top and sides of the body together, leaving a 2" (5 cm) opening for the head. Stuff the body, adding plastic beads to the bottom for weight and stability.
6. Whipstitch the head to the body.
7. Fold in two corners of the 2" x 2" square for the beak to create a piece 1¼" (3 cm) across. Fold in the other two corners and roll the piece up into a tight tube. Sew this tube closed at the end and along the length. Attach the open end to the head with the beak color.
8. Embroider eyes on the head with brown yarn. Weave in all ends.

Loon and Chick

No one is going to confuse this mama and baby loon with the real thing. For one thing, I don't believe that the real loon feather pattern runs to houndstooth, which is the weave you will use on the loon's body. To produce a houndstooth pattern, you have to wind and weave on the 4" x 6" pin loom in an unusual (but traditional) manner because the weave has two lines of white alternating with two lines of black in both the warp and weft. Complete directions for this weaving pattern are below.

Finished Measurements

Adult Loon: 7" x 8" (18 x 20 cm)
Chick: 5" x 5" (12.5 x 12.5 cm)

Tools

- 2" x 2" pin loom
- 2" x 4" pin loom
- 2" x 6" pin loom
- 4" x 6" pin loom
- Size G-6 (4.0 mm) crochet hook
- Tapestry needle

Yarn

Medium worsted (weight category 4) wool or acrylic-wool blend yarn

Adult Loon
- 50 yd. (46 m) black
- 31 yd. (28 m) white
- 3 yd. (2.7 m) charcoal gray
- Scrap amount (less than 1 ft. [30 cm]) red

Chick
- 29 yd. (27 m) heather gray
- 4 yd. (3.7 m) white
- Scrap amount (less than 1 ft. [30 cm]) black

Notions

- Polyester fiberfill
- Plastic pellets or small beans

Instructions

Adult Loon

NOTE: There are not separate patterns for male and female loons, as there are for the ducks, because adult loons all look exactly alike. So if you want to make an entire loon family, just do two of the adults and one or two chicks.

1. Weave:
   - Two 2" x 2" weavies in black
   - One 2" x 2" weavie in charcoal gray
   - One 2" x 4" weavie in white
   - One 2" x 2" weavie in black and white (wind in black and weave in white)
   - One 2" x 6" weavie in white and black (wind in white and weave in black)
   - Two 4" x 6" weavies in black and white (wind in black and weave in white)
   - Two 4" x 6" weavies in houndstooth pattern on at least half of each weavie (see sidebar)

WEAVING THE HOUNDSTOOTH PATTERN

The houndstooth pattern is created by alternating between two lines of white and two lines of black in both the warp (vertical strands) and weft (horizontal strands). Rather than following the normal process for weaving on a pin loom, wind all of the 6" warp strands in one layer, alternating a loop of white with a loop of black. You will then weave the 4" weft strands in the same way, weaving a strand of white across and back, then a strand of black across and back.

Since only about half of the weavie will show (the rest will be covered by the wings), you can choose to wind half of the warp with the alternating strands of white and black, and then switch to all black for the rest. Of course, if you prefer, you can just weave the whole square in the houndstooth pattern, as shown above.

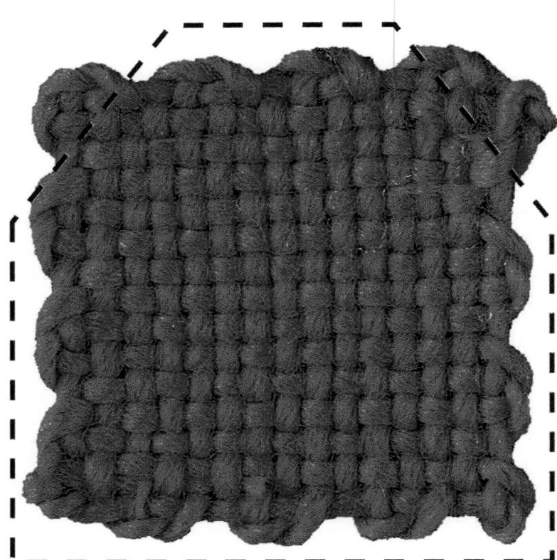

2. Single crochet around the edge of each of the 2" x 2" black weavies, folding in the top two corners and omitting the chain stitches on these corners (chain 2 in the bottom two corners as usual), as shown in the diagram. Whipstitch two pieces together and stuff. Half double crochet around the bottom edge of the head in white to make the neck. Add more stuffing to the neck.

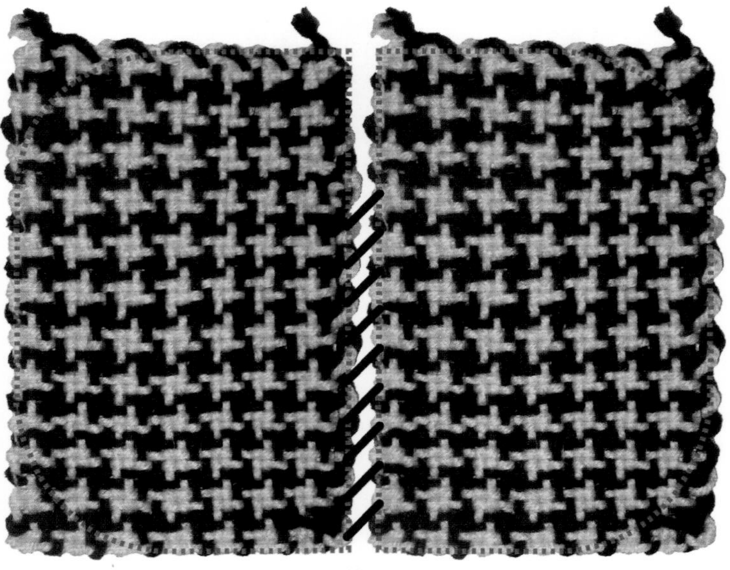

3. Using mattress stitch, join the two houndstooth-patterned 4" x 6" weavies along one long side for 4", leaving a 2" gap for the head. Turn under the corners, as shown in the diagram, and sc in black around the edge of the piece.

4. Single crochet around the edge of the white 2" x 4" weavie in white; this piece will form the chest.

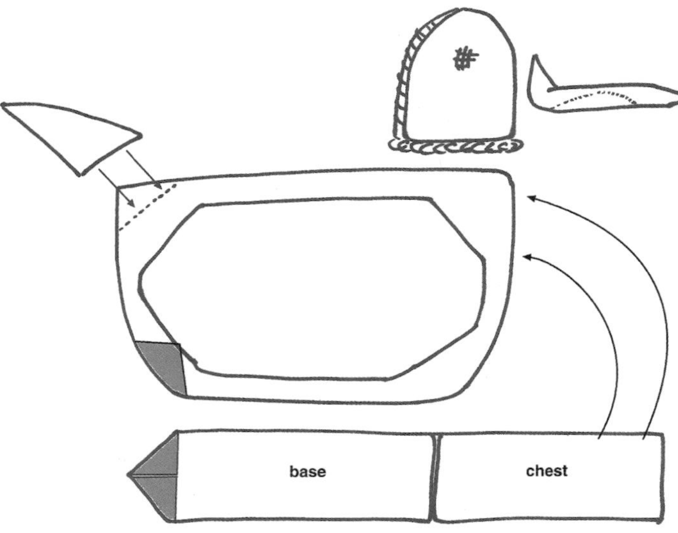

5. Turn under the corners on one narrow end of the 2" x 6" weavie to make a V. Single crochet around the edge of the piece in white; this piece is the base. Whipstitch the flat narrow end of the base to a narrow side of the chest, as shown in the diagram.
6. Line up the end of the chest with the front of the body, with the gap you left for the head at the same end as the chest. Whipstitch each side of the body to chest and base. Whipstitch the edges of the body together on the tail end. Add plastic pellets for stability, then stuff the piece.
7. Position head in the opening you left and whipstitch it in place.

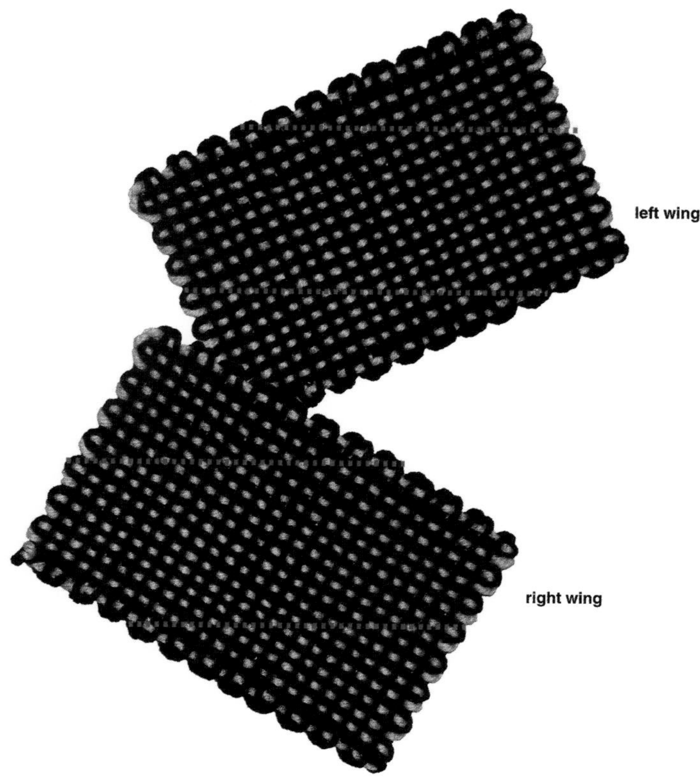

8. Fold each of the remaining 4" x 6" weavies into a wing shape as shown in the diagram. Since the dots on the wings are somewhat directional, orient the wings so that the directions of the dots mirror each other on the left and right wing. Sew the sides and bottom of each wing to the body, leaving the top open to add realism and because it makes a great pocket.
9. Single crochet around the edge of the black and white 2" x 2" weavie. Fold on diagonal and whipstitch one side of the triangle formed to make a cone. Stuff the cone, then place it on the tail end of the loon, more or less horizontally to help emphasize the loon's length.
10. Roll up the 2" x 2" gray weavie on the diagonal, so that there is a point at each end. Stitch this tube closed. Smash one pointed end up against loon head and sew it to the head with gray yarn. The beak should be long, pointed at the end, and canted slightly down.
11. Use red yarn to embroider eyes on each side of head. Weave in all ends.

Chick

1. Weave:
   - Four 2" x 2" weavies in gray
   - Two 2" x 4" weavies in gray
   - Two 2" x 2" weavies in gray and white (wind in gray; weave in white)
   - One 2" x 4" weavies in gray and white (wind in gray; weave in white)

NOTE: The loon chick's basic construction is the same as that of the duckling. Refer to the diagram on page 71 as you assemble the chick.

2. Single crochet around the edge of a gray 2" x 2" weavie, folding in the top two corners and omitting the extra chains at these corners (chain 2 at the other two corners as usual), as shown in the diagram. Repeat with second gray 2" x 2" weavie. Whipstitch the pieces together around three sides and stuff the piece.
3. Turn in the corners of the gray and white 2" x 4" weavie and single crochet around the edge in gray. Take the two gray 2" x 4" weavies for the sides of body, turn in the bottom two corners, and single crochet around the edge of each piece in gray. Whipstitch the body to the base, leaving a 2" opening for the head. Add pellets in the bottom of the body for stability, then stuff the rest of the way with fiberfill.
4. Insert the head into the opening and sew in place.
5. Single crochet around the edge of one of the gray 2" x 2" weavies. Fold three sides under and sew in place to form a flat tab. Attach to the back of the chick with the open corner pointed toward the head for a tail; the tail should be short, stubby, and horizontal.
6. Hold a gray and white 2" x 2" weavie on the diagonal and turn under the top and left corner to make a little wing; sew the wing to the left side of the body. Repeat on the other side with the top and right corners.
7. Take the remaining gray 2" x 2" weavie and roll diagonally as tightly as possible. Sew the roll closed, loop a piece of yarn around the tube about one-third of the way along, and tie tightly. Cut the tube just past the tie so that you have a piece about a third of the length that is tied off so it won't fall apart. Place the cut end against the head and sew in place.
8. Embroider an eye on each side of head in black. Weave in all ends.

CHAPTER 4

Blankets

Sweetheart Baby Blanket

The blanket is made with a heart pattern woven in some of its squares and finished with a sweet decorative crochet edging. The blanket is joined using the mattress stitch, a join that balances strength with speed. Since this is a baby blanket, consider using an easy-to-wash yarn. I used worsted-weight yarn in ecru and bright yellow, which produced a medium-weight cloth. Choose a light baby yarn for a thinner fabric with a more open weave. I've also included instructions for a matching ball and bonnet.

Finished Measurements

37" x 37" (94 x 94 cm)

Tools

- 4" x 4" pin loom
- 2" x 2" pin loom (used for the ball only)
- Size G-6 (4.0 mm) crochet hook
- Tapestry needle

Yarn

Medium worsted (weight category 4) yarn (sample made with Vanna's Choice Baby Yarn)

Blanket
- 495 yd. (453 m) ecru
- 144 yd. (132 m) yellow

Bonnet
- 30 yd. (27 m) ecru
- 2 yd. (1.8 m) yellow

Ball
- Total of 18 yd. (16 m) in one color or various colors

Notions

- Polyester fiberfill (for ball)

Instructions

Blanket

1. Weave:
   - Sixteen 4" x 4" yellow squares
   - Forty-nine 4" x 4" ecru squares
   - Sixteen 4" x 4" ecru squares in the heart pattern (see page 15)
2. Lay out the squares as shown in the diagram. Use the mattress stitch to join them together, first connecting the squares into strips, then sewing the strips together.
3. Hdc around the edge of the blanket with ecru yarn. This adds weight and color continuity. Do not break off the yarn at the end of the round.
4. Work a second round of crochet around the blanket as follows: Half double crochet, chain 4, skip next stitch; repeat this pattern all the way around the blanket. Add an extra 2 chains at each corner. At the end of the round, join the work with a slip stitch in the first stitch of the second round. Cut the yarn, fasten off, and weave in the ends.

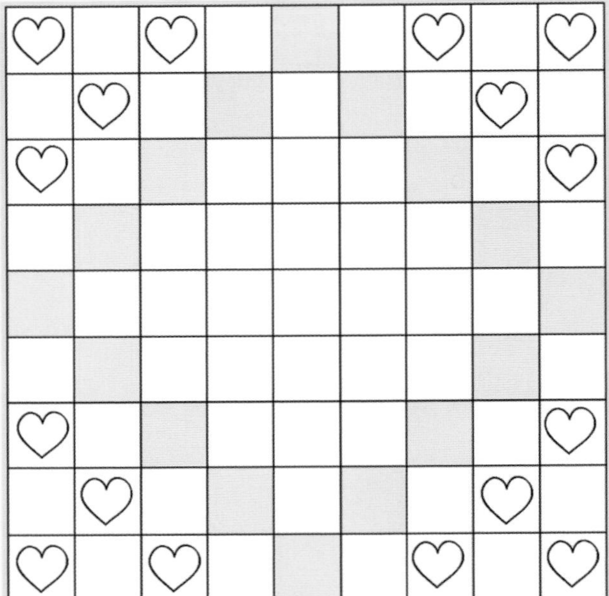

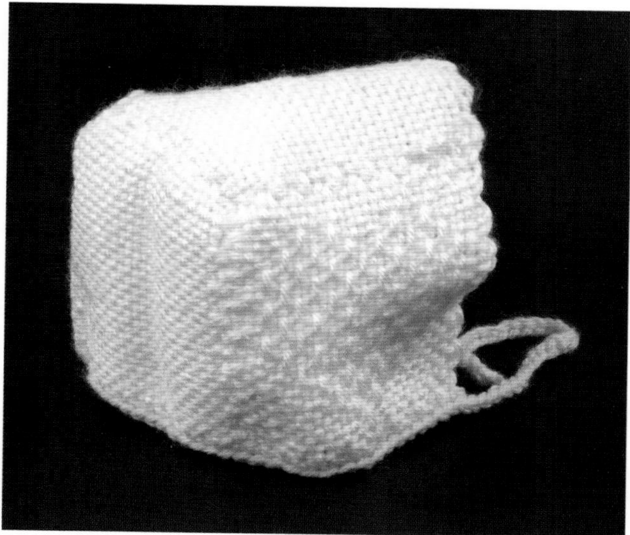

Bonnet

1. With ecru, weave two 4" x 4" plain weave squares and two in the heart pattern (see page 15).
2. Sew the squares together using mattress stitch as shown in the diagram. Fold squares together to form half a cube.
3. Using the yellow yarn, make a 6" (15 cm) chain. Continuing from this chain, work single crochet around the bottom edge of the bonnet. At the end of the bottom edge, work another 6" (15 cm) of chain to complete the bonnet ties. Fasten off and weave in ends.

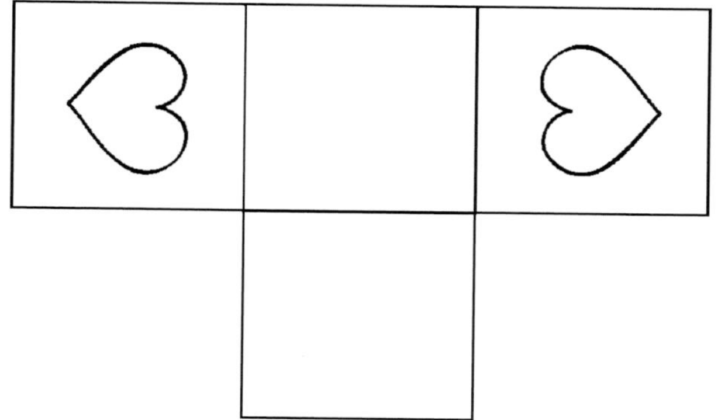

Ball

1. Weave six 2" x 2" squares (all in yellow or two each in three different colors).
2. Single crochet around the edge of each square in its own color.
3. Whipstitch the squares together as shown in the diagram to form a cube, leaving one side open.
4. Stuff the ball with with polyester stuffing, then sew the last side closed. Weave in all ends.

Red Squares Lap Blanket

This small blanket makes a great lap blanket or a blanket for a toddler. Like a quilt pattern, this blanket design lends itself to many colorways. The blanket shown here was assembled by adding a single crochet edge on each weavie and then whipstitching them together. I have also included the yarn amount needed for an alternate joining method (the double overcast stitch).

Finished Measurements

48" x 48" (120 x 120 cm)

Tools

- 2" x 2" pin loom
- 2" x 4" pin loom
- 2" x 6" pin loom
- 4" x 4" pin loom
- 4" x 6" pin loom
- 6" x 6" pin loom
- Size G-6 (4.0 mm) crochet hook
- Tapestry needle

Keep in mind that you can construct the more unusual sizes of weavies by joining smaller weavies—for example, joining several 2" x 2" squares to make a 2" x 6".

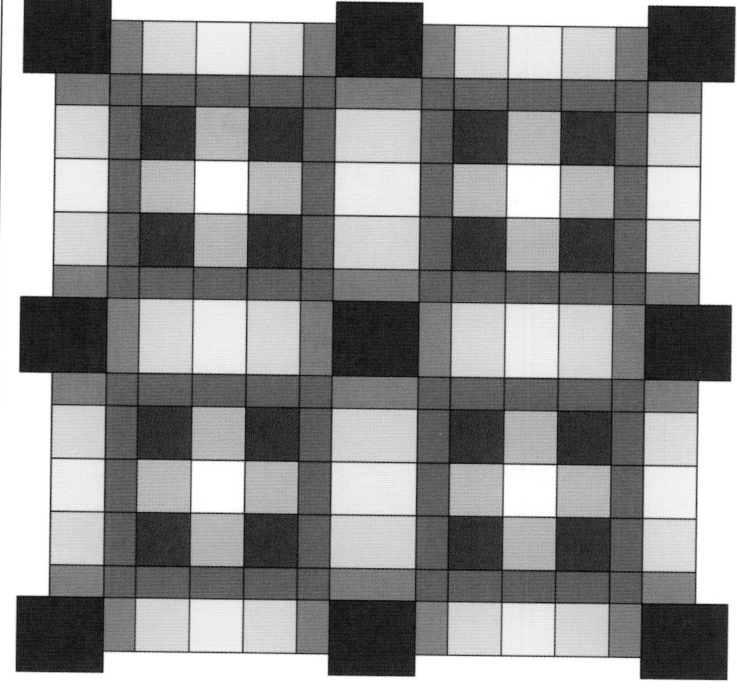

Yarn

Medium worsted (weight category 4) acrylic yarn
- 255 yd. (233 m) [215 yd. (197 m)] dark brown
- 148 yd. (135 m) [112 yd. (102 m)] medium brown
- 280 yd. (256 m) [208 yd. (190 m)] light brown
- 140 yd. (128 m) [104 yd. (95 m)] cream
- 377 yd. (345 m) [290 yd. (265 m)] red
- 160 yd. (146 m) [120 yd. (110 m)] charcoal
- 160 yd. (146 m) [120 yd. (110 m)] light gray
- 40 yd. (37 m) [30 yd. (27 m)] white

The main yarn amount given includes a crochet edging and whipstitching; the amounts in brackets are the amounts needed if joining with the double overcast stitch. Use a single yarn type for all colors to achieve the best drape.

Instructions

1. Weave:
   - Nine 6" x 6" weavies in dark brown
   - Eight 2" x 6" weavies in medium brown
   - Sixteen 2" x 4" weavies in medium brown
   - Eight 4" x 6" weavies in light brown
   - Sixteen 4" x 4" weavies in light brown
   - Four 4" x 6" weavies in cream
   - Eight 4" x 4" weavies in cream
   - Sixteen 2" x 2" weavies in red
   - Forty-eight 2" x 4" weavies in red
   - Sixteen 4" x 4" weavies in charcoal
   - Sixteen 4" x 4" weavies in light gray
   - Four 4" x 4" weavies in white
2. Single crochet around the edge of each weavie in its own color, remembering to chain 2 at each corner.
3. Arrange the weavies as shown in the chart.
4. Whipstitch the weavies together. (Or skip the crochet edge and sew the weavies together with the double overcast stitch.)
5. Single crochet around the assembled blanket in dark brown; work a second row of single crochet around the edge in red. Weave in all ends.

Variation

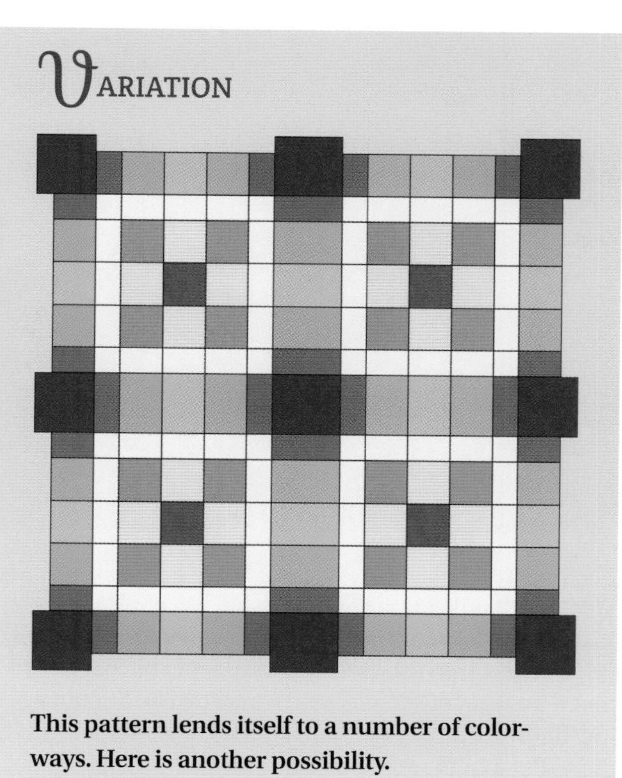

This pattern lends itself to a number of colorways. Here is another possibility.

Spring Colors Blanket

This blanket was made in a soft, washable wool yarn. I wanted it to be big enough to throw across a bed or to use as a cozy wrap for two. That means that it has a lot of squares in it, which can be discouraging. But work on it slowly and steadily, and you will get there. Pin looms are so portable that many people find it easy to finish a few in waiting rooms or during their commute (unless you drive—I would not suggest trying to weave while you drive!). A few squares here and there adds up to a lot, in time. My suggested joining method breaks the assembly down into nine-square blocks. This makes it a less daunting task and makes it much easier to keep the blocks and corners aligned.

Finished Measurements

62" x 74" (163 x 188 cm)

Tools

- 4" x 4" hand loom
- Size G-6 (4.0 mm) crochet hook
- Tapestry needle

Yarn

Medium worsted (weight category 4) superwash wool yarn

- 665 yd. (608 m) yellow
- 780 yd. (713 m) white
- 450 yd. (411 m) dark teal
- 400 yd. (366 m) light teal

Instructions

1. Weave the following squares on the 4" x 4" pin loom:
   - Seventy-five yellow squares
   - Seventy-five white squares
   - Sixty dark teal squares
   - Thirty light teal squares
   - Thirteen teal and white striped squares (wind first two layers in light teal; wind the third layer and weave with white)
   - Four teal squares woven with white (wind three layers with light teal; weave with white)
   - Thirteen white squares woven with teal (wind three layers with white; weave with light teal)
2. Lay the squares out in nine-square groups. Using the dominant color in the group (yellow or white), sew the squares together with double overcast stitch. Single crochet around edge of the block in the same color as used for joining. This is a good time to clean up the back, weaving in and trimming yarn ends.
3. After the thirty 9-block squares are completed, lay them out as shown in the diagram and whipstitch the squares together using light teal yarn.
4. Single crochet around the outer edge of the blanket in light teal yarn. Weave in all ends.

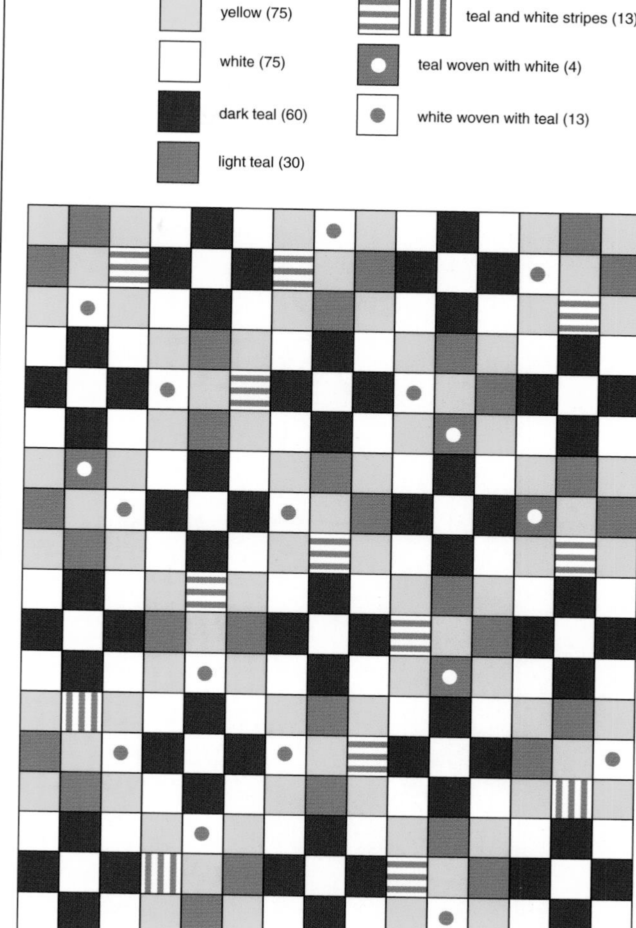

Variation

Instead of assembling the weavies in 9-block squares first, lay out all 270 squares at once and assemble them with the double overcast stitch—first joining the squares into strips, then attaching the rows together. Finish with a round of single crochet around the edge in white, then one round of light teal.

Blessing Path Toddler Blanket

If you weave for any length of time, some of the weaving will be for others. For me, the one occasion that is important enough to call for a blanket is the birth of a child. My preference is to make a blanket that is big enough to see a child through his or her first several years rather than just the infancy. This works well for two reasons. First, toddler blankets can be much more varied and creative; second, this gives you a good year or two to make it. This blanket makes a particularly good gift because, like the Sweetheart Baby Blanket, it is assembled using the mattress stitch, which means it goes together very quickly. It is a great way to send love and blessings to a new little person. My example shows a blessing from St. Clare. Consider stitching in your own best thoughts or prayers for a very personal, loving gift.

Finished Measurements

Approximately 36" x 44" (90 x 110 cm)

Tools

- 4" x 4" pin loom
- Size G-6 (4.0 mm) crochet hook
- Tapestry needle
- Washable pastel marker to sketch in words (optional)

Yarn

Medium worsted (weight category 4) acrylic yarn
- 90 yd. (82 m) pink
- 350 yd. (320 m) berry
- 325 yd. (297 m) wheat
- 40 yd. (37 m) grape
- 12 yd. (11 m) charcoal or black

The blanket pictured here was made using Red Heart Soft yarn for ease of care.

Instructions

1. On the 4" x 4" loom, weave:
   - Twelve squares in pink in the five-star pattern (see page 17)
   - Forty-five squares in berry in the one-star pattern (see page 18)
   - Forty-two squares in tan in plain weave
2. Lay out the squares as shown in the diagram. Keep in mind that the star patterns are not in the exact middles of the squares (because the squares have an even number of threads, so there is no exact middle thread). If you want them to all look the same, make sure you place them all on the same axis.
3. Join the tan squares using mattress stitch and tan yarn. Join the pink and berry border pieces and attach the sections of the blanket together with mattress stitch and berry yarn.

> **VARIATION**
>
> **This blanket could also serve as lap blanket. A friend of mine has made several in this style for relatives, embellishing them with the recipients' favorite hymns or verses.**

> **VARIATIONS**
>
> **This little blanket would work in a number of colorways. Look for three colors that go together well: a light color for the blocks of text and a medium and a dark shade for the edging. You could also use a dark color for the boxes and stitch the words on in tan or white, and use a light and a medium for the edging.**

4. Sketch in the words with washable pastel marker. Using running stitch, embroider text on the tan squares with charcoal or black yarn. Don't be too fastidious about letter placement; this is a piece that will improve with imperfection.
5. Run cold water over the pieces to wash off the marker and let dry. Finish assembling the blanket with mattress stitch and berry yarn.
6. Work a round of single crochet around the edge of the blanket in grape. At the end of the round, join with a slip stitch in the first stitch, then fasten off. Weave in ends.

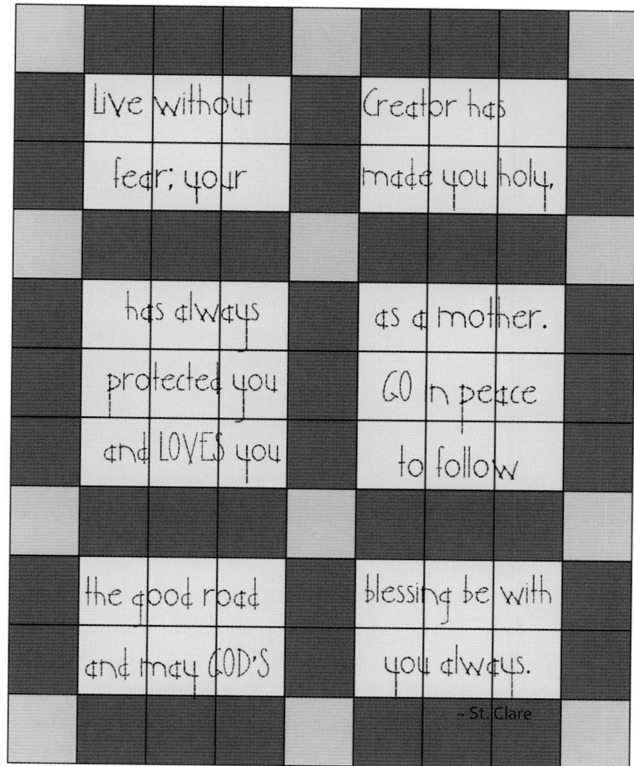

Animals Toddler Blanket

Much like a mother talking about a favorite child, I am a little embarrassed to admit that this may be my very favorite piece. It has a soft, textured edging, brought about by use of a patterned weave, and very simple, eye catching illustrations. My intention was to use pictures and colors that related as much to boys as girls. You can use the drawings that accompany the pattern or substitute any simple coloring book–style drawing. The illustrations are not difficult to do, they are primarily accomplished with crochet slip stitch and free stitching. Since this item would likely be given to a toddler, I would suggest using easy-to-wash yarns.

Finished Measurements

Approximately 40" x 48" (100 x 120 cm)

Tools

- 4" x 4" pin loom
- 4" x 6" pin loom
- 6" x 6" pin loom
- Size G-6 (4.0 mm) crochet hook
- Size 5 (1.9 mm) steel crochet hook (optional)
- Tapestry needle

Yarn

Medium worsted (weight category 4) acrylic yarn

- 370 yd. (338 m) light brown
- 208 yd. (190 m) mustard
- 315 yd. (288 m) ecru
- 40 yd. (37 m) black

Notions

- One ball of black crochet thread, size 10

Instructions

1. Weave:
    - Forty-two 4" x 4" ecru weavies
    - Thirty-two 4" x 6" light brown weavies using the eight-rib pattern (see page 16)
    - Two 4" x 4" light brown weavies
    - Nineteen 4" x 4" mustard weavies
    - Four 6" x 6" mustard weavies
2. Lay the ecru weavies out in six blocks—four blocks that are two squares by three squares and two blocks that are three squares by three squares. Use the double overcast stitch and ecru yarn to join the squares.
3. Using a washable pen, transfer the illustrations onto the ecru blocks. There are several approaches you can use. You can place the illustration underneath the cloth and use a light table or window to trace the drawing. You can also use a pattern tracer, perforating the illustration and marking it onto the cloth with a washable marker or colored chalk.
4. Using black crochet thread and the size G-6 crochet hook, follow the main lines of the illustration in slip stitch (see page 19). Use the smaller crochet hook to pull the crochet thread through tight spaces. It can get pretty tangled underneath the illustration. Leave some long strings on the back so that you can secure and trim the threads at the end.
5. Add details using a free stitch with tapestry needle. This is one of the places where less is more. You might notice that there are a lot of details in the illustrations that never made it onto the blanket pictured here. Use as little or as much detail as you choose.
6. Using the light brown yarn, add some patches of light brown to the giraffe with irregular cross-stitches. You can add more color to any of the other drawings as you choose.

TIP: Keep in mind that if you don't want to get a 6" x 6" loom, you can build this square from other sizes, overlapping and sewing together several 4" x 4" or 4" x 6" weavies.

7. Assemble the blanket using the double overcast stitch. Use light brown yarn on any seam that goes along a light brown edge. Use mustard gold yarn for all the other seams.
8. Single crochet around the edge of the blanket in black yarn. At the end of the round, join with a slip stitch in the first stitch and fasten off. Weave in ends.

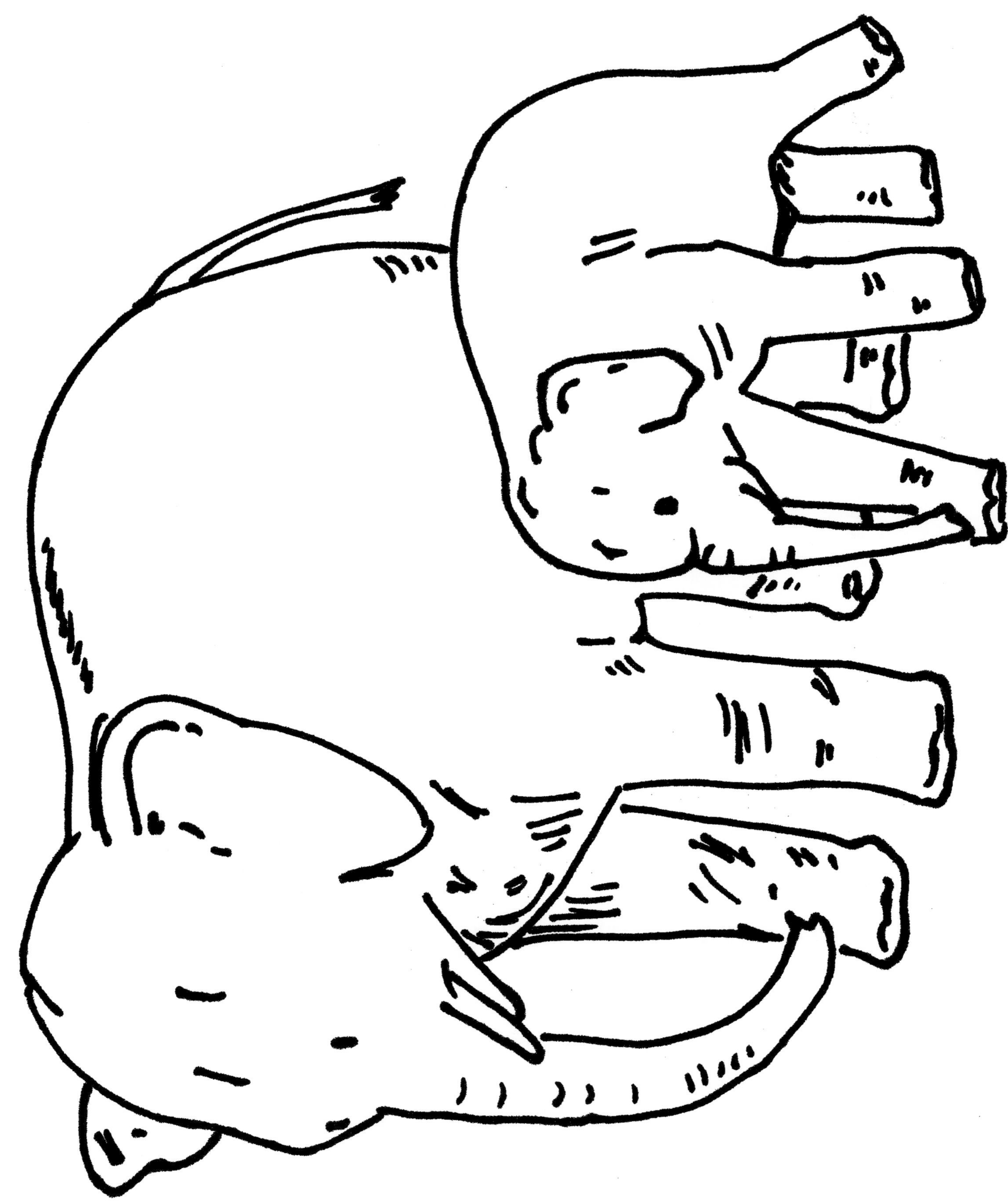

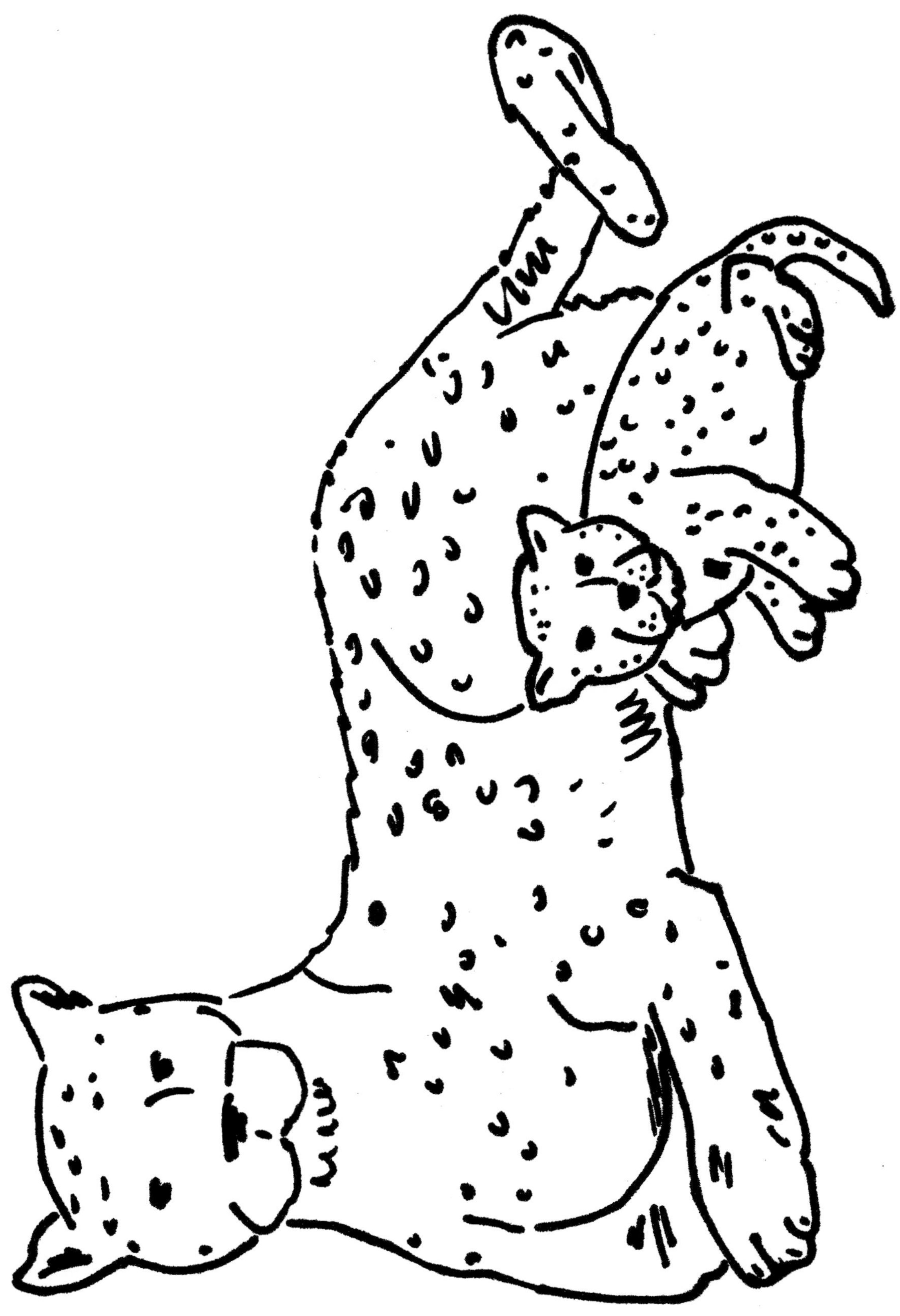

Checkerboard Blanket

This blanket was intended to reproduce the look of an old checkerboard painted on wood surrounded by a primitive illustration of barns, houses, grass, and sky. While the dimensions of the checkerboard itself are fixed, the approach you take to the surrounding illustration can vary. Keep in mind that the checkerboard squares have a single crochet border, which makes each of those squares just a little wider (but neater and better defined) than the squares in the decorative border. You will need more squares in the grass and sky parts to equal the dimensions of the checkerboard. The reason for changing to the more willy-nilly approach in the border is that it gives a primitive, pieced look. The diagram has dotted lines to show where the separate weavies connect. Keep in mind that it is an approximation and is not to scale. You may find that you need to overlap squares at some points in the sky and grass sections to make a good fit.

All the weavies representing sky and grass are woven with two yarns, a thick, soft, variegated yarn for the first layer and a thinner, sturdier, easier to weave worsted wool for the rest. This means that they are all somewhat dotted and each square is a bit different. The blue variegated yarn was so soft that some of its fiber that did not get entirely picked up in the weaving on the back side. I turned the blue weavies over to give a look of fleecy clouds.

My directions suggest completely assembling the blanket before doing any embroidery or embellishment. That is because the weavies gain structure and stability as they are joined. However, you might prefer to work on some of the elements separately because they can be easier to handle that way. For example, you may want to put the houses and barn together and add the window elements before connecting them to the rest of the project.

Finished Measurements

36" x 48" (91 x 122 cm)

Tools

- 4" x 4" pin loom
- 2" x 2" pin loom
- Size G-6 (4.0 mm) crochet hook
- Tapestry needle

Yarn

Bulky (weight category 5) yarn in variegated green and blue; medium worsted (weight category 4) yarn for all other colors

Blanket

- 136 yd. (124 m) variegated green
- 116 yd. (106 m) variegated blue
- 1170 yd. (1070 m) natural
- 320 yd. (293 m) teal
- 40 yd. (37 m) brick red
- 64 yd. (59 m) light coral
- 64 yd. (59 m) cream
- 60 yd. (55 m) black heather
- 136 yd. (124 m) charcoal gray
- 8 yd. (7.3 m) light gray
- 6 yd. (5.5 m) yellow
- 30 yd. (27 m) dark brown
- 10 yd. (9 m) light brown
- 5 yd. (4.6 m) light green
- Scrap amount (less than 1 yd. [0.9 m]) of fuchsia or dark pink

Checkers

- 60 yd. (55 m) natural
- 60 yd. (55 m) teal

Notions

- Plastic beads or lentils

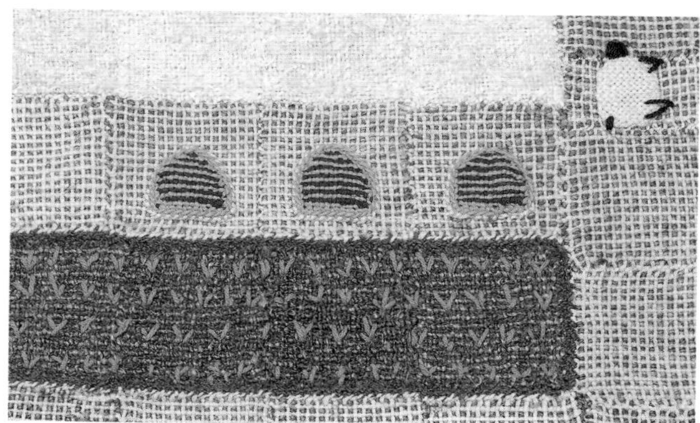

Instructions

1. Weave the following squares on the 4" x 4" loom:
   - Thirty-two squares in natural
   - Thirty-two squares in teal
   - Five squares in brick red
   - Eight squares in coral
   - Eight squares in cream
   - Eight squares in black heather
   - Five squares in charcoal gray
   - One square in brown
   - Fifty-eight squares with the first layer in variegated blue and the others in natural
   - Sixty-four squares with the first layer in variegated green and the others in natural
   - Four squares with the first two layers in variegated green and the other two in brown

   Weave the following squares on the 2" x 2" loom:
   - Two squares in light gray
   - Four squares in charcoal gray
   - Three squares with the first two layers in yellow and the other two in brown
   - Eight squares in natural
2. Single crochet around the edges of the thirty-two teal and thirty-two natural squares (teal on the teal squares and natural on the natural ones). Whipstitch the squares together in a checkerboard pattern. Single crochet around the edge of the checkerboard with natural yarn.
3. Join the variegated blue squares together in strips using natural yarn and the double overcast stitch. Use the double overcast stitch to attach the blue strips around the checkerboard. You may have to overlap a blue square on each side to match the size of the checkerboard exactly.
4. Join the coral and cream squares to construct the houses. For the roofs, lay one variegated green/natural 4" x 4" square on top of a black 4" x 4" square. Sew them together on the diagonal, then open up the piece so that the two black triangles are on one side of the seam and the two green triangles are on the other. This square is one half of the house gable for the cream-colored house. Match up and complete the other

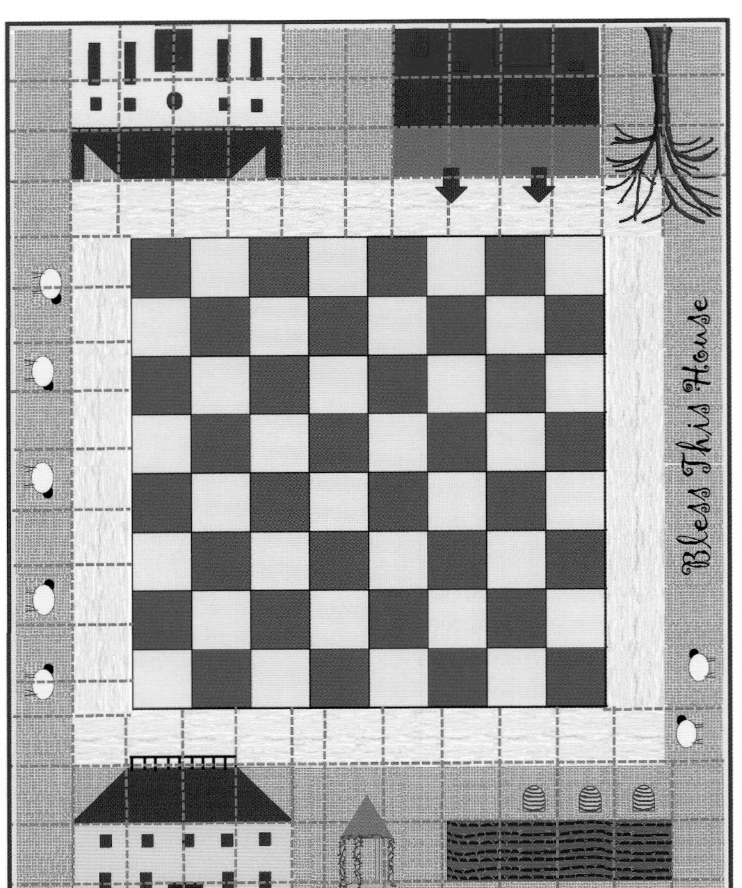

gable squares (two for each house) in the same way. The coral-colored house has a charcoal roof and the cream-colored house has a black roof. Lay out all the roof squares and join using double overcast stitch in the matching yarn color.

5. Join the four variegated green/brown squares and single crochet around the edge of the block in brown; this represents a garden.
6. Following the diagram, lay out the squares and join, using double overcast stitch and natural, to complete the fabric of the blanket.
7. Single crochet in natural around the edge of the blanket, then add a second row of single crochet in charcoal.
8. Create the remaining elements and appliqué them onto the decorative border:
   - Bee skeps: Single crochet in yellow around the three brown and yellow 2" x 2" squares. Omit the corner chains in the top corners and turn the corners under to round off the tops of the squares.
   - Barn cupolas: Fold two charcoal gray 2" x 2" squares on the diagonal. Fold the edges of the other two dark gray 2" x 2" squares in slightly to make columns about 1¼" (3 cm) wide. Stitch these pieces in place on the top of the barn, sticking up onto the sky squares.
   - Sheep: Fold in the corners of eight 2" x 2" natural squares and stitch them down as sheep. Add tiny heads and legs using satin stitch in charcoal gray.
   - Garden folly: Fold a dark gray 4" x 4" square into a triangular shape for the roof. Join two light gray 2" x 2" squares for the base. Add columns in satin stitch to complete the garden folly.
   - Front doors: Fold one brick red 4" x 4" square to make a piece approximately 3" x 4" and stitch it in place on the cream-colored house. Do the same with a brown square for the coral-colored house.
9. Embroider any additional details on the piece. Use satin stitch and dark gray yarn to add the windows to the houses. Add any other house features desired, including the widow's walk on top of the coral house. Use brown or gray yarn to add a tree to the corner of the blanket. Use light green yarn to add plants in the garden and climbing vines on the folly. Add dots of dark pink to the folly to represent roses.
10. Embroider words in running stitch on one side of blanket. You can follow the suggested wording in the diagram or personalize it—for example, "The Miller Plantation." You can print out your planned wording in your choice of font and sketch in the words with washable pastel marker. The font used in the diagram is called Gigi. Run cold water over the area to wash off the marker after you have embroidered the letters. Weave in all ends.

Checkers

Weave twelve plain 2" x 2" squares and twelve patterned 2" x 2" squares (see weaving pattern below) in each color (teal and natural). Line up a patterned square with a plain one of the same color, right sides out, and single crochet edge in the same color. Stop about 1" (2.5 cm) from the end and add about a teaspoon of plastic beads or small beans such as lentils before closing the playing piece. Weave in all ends. The patterned side of each piece is the "king" side.

CHECKERS WEAVING PATTERN

Row 1: Weave plain.
Row 2: W6, U3, W6.
Row 3: W4, U3, O1, U3, W4.
Row 4: W2, U3, O1, U3, O1, U3, W2.
Row 5: W4, U3, O1, U3, W4.
Row 6: W6, U3, W6.
Row 7: Weave plain.
Row 8: Weave plain.

Parcheesi Blanket

The Parcheesi board has been tempting me for years. Every time I saw the colors and all the shapes and squares, I wanted to turn it into a blanket where you could play a game with the family while keeping your legs warm. My dream has finally come true. (However, I have found that you have to choose either to play Parcheesi on it or to use it as a lap robe. If you try to do both at once, the kids will say that you're cheating.)

The muted colors of this design were intended to evoke an earlier time when winter evenings were spent playing games with family and friends. The directions for making the playing pieces and the dice follow the blanket directions. You may need to look in Great-grandma's attic or check online for the rules of the game.

Finished Measurements

54" x 54" (137 x 137 cm)

Tools

- 2" x 2" pin loom
- 4" x 4" pin loom
- 2" x 4" pin loom
- 6" x 6" pin loom
- Size G-6 (4.0 mm) crochet hook
- Tapestry needle

Yarn

Medium worsted (weight category 4) wool-mohair blend yarn (sample made with Lamb's Pride worsted, 85% wool, 15% mohair)

Gameboard
- 243 yd. (222 m) maroon
- 207 yd. (189 m) blue
- 207 yd. (189 m) yellow
- 183 yd. (167 m) green
- 24 yd. (22 m) red
- 373 yd. (341 m) taupe
- 240 yd. (219 m) dark red
- 240 yd. (219 m) dark blue
- 35 yd. (32 m) sky blue
- 36 yd. (33 m) dark gray
- 454 yd. (415 m) dark brown
- Scrap amount (less than 1 yd. [0.9 m]) white

Playing Pieces
- 40 yd. (37 m) maroon yarn
- 40 yd. (37 m) blue yarn
- 40 yd. (37 m) yellow yarn
- 40 yd. (37 m) green yarn

Dice
- 18 yd. (16 m) yarn per die (your choice of one or several colors)
- Scrap amount of contrasting-color yarn

Notions

- Plastic pellets or small beans
- Polyester fiberfill

Instructions

Gameboard

1. Weave:
   - Eighteen 4" x 4" weavies in maroon
   - One 6" x 6" weavie in maroon
   - Two 2" x 2" weavies in maroon
   - Eighteen 4" x 4" weavies in blue
   - One 6" x 6" weavie in blue
   - Two 2" x 2" weavies in blue
   - Eighteen 4" x 4" weavies in yellow
   - One 6" x 6" weavie in yellow
   - Two 2" x 2" weavies in yellow
   - Eighteen 4" x 4" weavies in green
   - One 6" x 6" weavie in green
   - Two 2" x 2" weavies in green
   - One 6" x 6" weavie in red
   - One 2" x 2" weavie in red
   - Forty-eight 2" x 4" weavies in dark brown
   - Sixteen 2" x 2" weavies in taupe
   - Thirty-two 4" x 4" weavies in taupe
   - Twenty-four 4" x 4" weavies in dark red
   - Twenty-four 4" x 4" weavies in dark blue
   - One 2" x 4" weavie in dark blue
   - Two 4" x 4" weavies in sky blue
   - Five 2" x 2" weavies in sky blue
   - Three 4" x 4" weavies in dark gray
   - Six 4" x 4" weavies with the first three layers in maroon and the last layer woven in taupe
2. Single crochet around the edge of each weavie in its own color—except for two of the dark gray weavies and two of the sky blue 4" x 4" weavies.
3. Lay one of the sky blue weavies without edging on top of one of the dark gray ones. Sew them together on the diagonal, then open up the piece so that the two blue triangles are on one side of the seam and the two gray triangles are on the other. This square represents one half of the roof line. Single crochet around the square with blue on the blue half and gray on the gray half. Repeat with the other pair of un-edged weavies.

Making the Home Square

4. Using dark gray yarn, whipstitch the gray square and the two gray and blue pieces you made in step 3 together into a strip, with the sky blue parts on the ends. This will be the roof of the house and part of the sky: Check the diagram to make sure that the roof line matches and the diagonal squares are set in the right direction.
5. Using maroon yarn, whipstitch the six maroon/taupe 4" x 4" squares in a two-by-three block to represent the house. Using dark gray yarn, whipstitch the house to the roof.

6. Using maroon yarn, whipstitch the additional decorative elements onto the house: the dark blue 2" x 4" weavie (to represent the door) and the five sky blue 2" x 2" squares (for the windows). Add simple backstitch or running stitch to the windows in dark gray to indicate the panes.
7. Using white or taupe yarn, stitch the word "HOME" on the roof of the house with a slip stitch.

Making the Medallion Squares

8. Whipstitch nine 4" x 4" squares of blue into a three-by-three block.
9. On top of this block stack the 6" x 6" yellow square, a 4" x 4" blue square, and a 2" x 2" yellow square. Orient these squares as shown in the diagram, with each square placed diagonal to the one directly below it. Whipstitch each square in place, using the opposite color (so the yellow squares are sewn on in blue, and the blue squares are sewn on in yellow).
10. Whipstitch three 2" x 4" dark brown weavies together end to end. Create three more strips in this way. Whipstitch one of these strips to one side of the medallion. Repeat on the opposite side. Whipstitch a 2" x 2" taupe weavie to each end of both of the remaining dark brown strips. Whipstitch these longer strips to the remaining open sides of the medallion. You should end up with the medallion is enclosed by a strip of dark brown weavies on each side with taupe squares in the corners.
11. Repeat steps 8–10 using the maroon and light blue weavies, the green and red weavies, and the yellow and red weavies.

Making the Paths Between the Medallions

12. Using dark brown yarn, whipstitch four taupe 4" x 4" weavies together into a strip. Repeat to make another strip of four taupe 4" x 4" weavies.

13. Using dark brown yarn, whipstitch four blue weavies together into a strip. Place the blue strip of weavies between the two strips of taupe weavies and whipstitch the three strips together side to side.
14. In order to create the correct number of game board spaces, each of the 4" x 4" weavies needs to have a line through drawn through it. Add this line using crochet slip stitch in dark brown yarn. You should end up with eight steps on each strip, as shown in the diagram.
15. Add the 2" x 2" blue weavie to this block, as shown in the diagram. Turn the weavie on the diagonal and turn the top and bottom corners under so that it fits in the 2" space. Whipstitch in place using dark brown yarn. This is the marker to indicate where game pieces enter the game.
16. Repeat steps 12–15 with maroon, yellow, and green weavies to construct the other three paths.

Assembling the Board and Border

17. Lay out the Home block, the four medallion blocks, and the four path blocks as shown in the diagram. Whipstitch all the blocks together using dark brown yarn with one exception: Use taupe yarn to join the taupe corners of the medallions to the taupe path blocks.
18. Whipstitch six dark blue and five dark red 4" x 4" squares together into a strip, alternating the colors (each strip should start and end with a dark blue square). Repeat to make a second strip. Whipstitch these strips to two opposite sides of the game board.
19. Whipstitch six dark blue and seven dark red 4" x 4" squares together into a strip, alternating the colors (each strip should start and end with a dark red square). Repeat to make a second strip. Whipstitch these strips to the remaining sides.
20. Work two rounds of half double crochet in dark brown around the edge of the blanket. Weave in all ends.

Playing Pieces

1. Weave four 4" x 4" squares in each color.
2. Single crochet around each square in its own color.
3. Bend the corners of a square up to meet, like you're building a little four-sided pyramid.
4. Whipstitch three pairs of sides together. Fill the piece with plastic pellets or dry beans such as lentils or small navy beans. Whipstitch the final pair of sides together to close the piece.
5. Repeat for the other fifteen pieces. Weave in all ends.

Dice

1. Weave six 2" x 2" squares in your choice of colors.
2. Single crochet around each 2" x 2" square in its own color.
3. Embroider dots on the pieces using contrasting-color yarn.
4. Whipstitch the squares together as shown in the diagram to form a cube. Stop before you whipstitch the last side closed.
5. Stuff firmly with polyester fiberfill, then finish closing the die. Weave in all ends.

CHAPTER FIVE

Farm Set

This farm set—a house or barn tote along with some matching people and farm animals—would be a great gift for a little boy or girl. It would be even more memorable if you were able to introduce them to small loom weaving so that they could carry the memories of your time and attention, of working one on one with you, into their adult life.

Amish Dolls

These little Amish dolls are surprisingly easy to make and you may find more and more demands for them. People are delighted with their simplicity: The dolls are made entirely out of weavies except for a few chenille sticks. You can find little hats, baskets, and tools for them to carry at craft stores.

Finished Measurements

6" (15 cm)

Tools

- 2" x 2" pin loom
- 4" x 4" pin loom
- 2" x 4" pin loom
- Size G-6 (4.0 mm) crochet hook
- Tapestry needle

Yarn

Doll

- 16 yd. (15 m) pink, tan, or brown light worsted (weight category 3) yarn (for skin color)

Girl's Clothing

Medium worsted (weight category 4) yarn

- 20 yd. (18 m) navy
- 7 yd. (6 m) white
- 7 yd. (6 m) light gray

Boy's Clothing

Medium worsted (weight category 4) yarn

- 16 yd. (15 m) navy

Notions

- Chenille sticks
- Polyester fiberfill

Instructions

Doll

1. Weave:
   - Four 2" x 2" weavies
   - Three 2" x 4" weavies

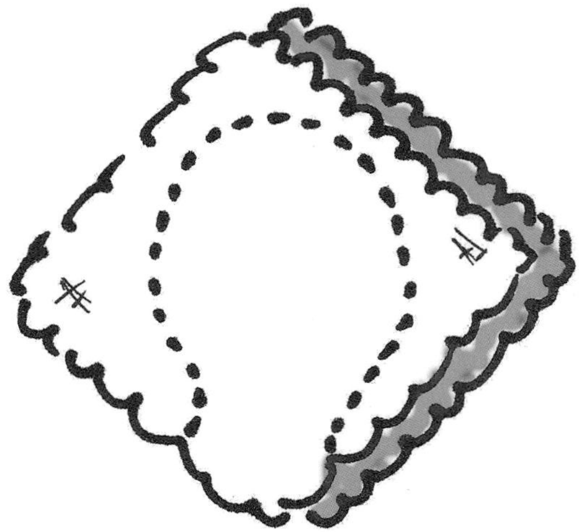

2. For the head and neck, take two 2" x 2" weavies and sew a circle in them in running stitch, using the same color yarn and leaving one corner open. Turn the piece inside out and add a little stuffing; it should be about the size of your thumb. Cut a 3" (7.5 cm) piece of chenille stick and stick it into the head stuffing to give more rigidity to the neck.
3. For the body, take a 2" x 4" weavie and single crochet around the edge in the same color. Fold this piece in half with the fold on one side of the body and place the head and neck piece in the middle of the top edge. Whipstitch around the top and side of the folded piece, securing the head in the body. Stuff the body.
4. For the legs, take two 2" x 4" weavies. Measure and cut two 8" (20 cm) chenille sticks and fold them in half. Roll up a doubled chenille stick in one 2" x 4" weavie and stitch along the length of the rolled-up weavie to secure it. Repeat for the second leg. Place the legs in the opening at the bottom of the body, adding stuffing as needed to fill up the bottom of the body, and whipstitch along the bottom edge of the body, sewing through the legs to secure them. Close the ends of the legs with a few overcast stitches in matching yarn for bare feet (the stitches give the appearance of toes), or use black yarn wrapped around the bottom of legs for shoes.
5. For the arms, measure and cut two 4" (10 cm) chenille sticks and fold them in half. Roll up a doubled chenille stick in one 2" x 2" weavie and sew along the length of the rolled-up weavie to secure it. Repeat this process for the second arm. Place one end of the arm flush against the doll's shoulder and use an overcast stitch all the way around the top of the arm to secure it. Repeat with the second arm. Close the ends of the arms with a few small overcast stitches in matching yarn; leave the loops of the weavie extending beyond the closure to give the look of fingers. Weave in all ends.
6. Use a tapestry needle or small crochet hook to add little loops of yarn to the head for hair. Take a length of yarn and secure it under the doll's scalp. Work overcast stitches over the doll's head, but do not draw the stitches tight; the loops left behind will look like very curly hair.

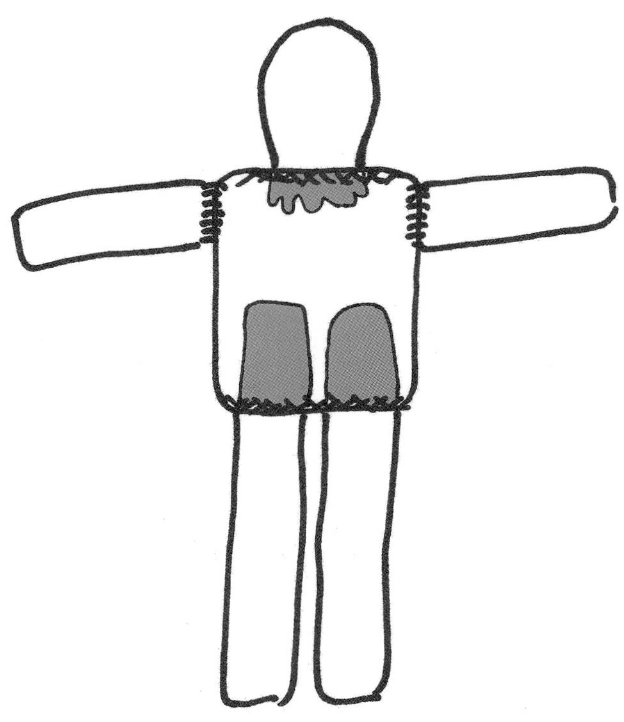

Variation

You can make a doll with "built in" clothes by changing up the colors of the weavies.

- **To add a shirt or undershirt, make the 2" x 4" weavie for the body in another color. You can give the shirt long sleeves by making the two 2" x 2" weavies for the arms in the shirt color. Close the ends of the arms in the skin color for hands. (You should do this for the Amish boy doll, as he only has a separate pattern for pants. You may want to give the Amish girl doll arms that match her dress color.)**
- **Give the doll stockings by making the 2" x 4" weavies for the legs in white or black. Close off the ends with the same color (or with black or brown for shoes).**

Girl's Clothing

1. Weave:
   - Two 4" x 4" weavies in navy
   - One 2" x 2" weavie in white
   - One 2" x 4" weavie in white
   - One 2" x 2" weavie in light gray
   - One 2" x 4" weavie in light gray
2. To make the dress: Join the two navy 4" x 4" weavies together using the mattress stitch. Single crochet around this rectangle. Add a 1" (2.5 cm) wide tab of double crochet in the middle of one long side of the dress. Wrap dress around the doll figure, with the tab of double crochet in the front. Add straps made from navy yarn going from the front of the dress to cross in the back to secure it. The straps can be tied or stitched in place.
3. To make the apron: Lay the 2" x 2" white weavie in the middle of the longer side of the 2" x 4" white weavie with a 1" (2.5 cm) overlap, and sew in place. Add yarn ties to the corners of the 2" x 4" weavie to complete the apron. Tie the apron around the doll's middle (or sew it in place if you prefer).

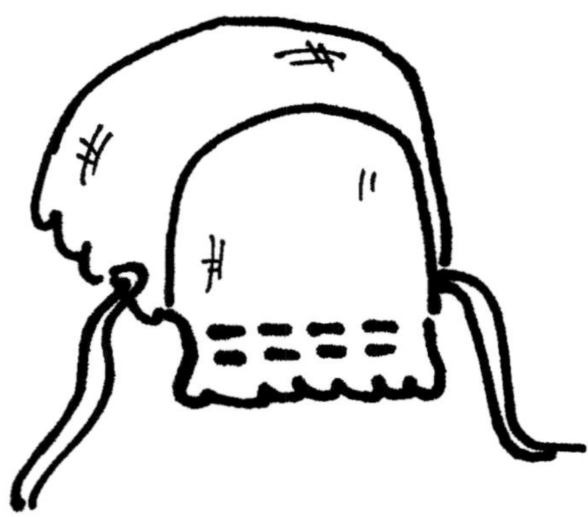

4. To make the bonnet: Center the 2" x 2" gray weavie in the middle of the longer side of the 2" x 4" weavie with almost no overlap and sew them together. Bring the sides of the 2" x 4" weavie down to meet the sides of the 2" x 2" weavie and sew them together to make the bonnet. The bottom of the 2" x 2" weavie should extend below the seam; this will be the bonnet's neck ruffle. Add a line of running stitches along the top of the ruffle and gather it just slightly to make it formfitting. Weave in all ends.

Boy's Clothing

1. Weave two 4" x 4" weavies in navy.
2. Place the weavies together and sew them together for 1¾" (4.5 cm) on opposite sides with a ¾" (2 cm) seam allowance. Open the piece up and flatten it out halfway so the seams go right up the middle. Sew the edges of each weavie together up to the seams previously made to form two pant legs. Turn the piece right side out. Single crochet around the edge at waist and and the bottoms of the legs.

3. Double a piece of navy or black yarn and weave it through the single crochet at the waist to tie as a belt. Put the pants on the doll and add yarn suspenders that cross in back. Weave in all ends.

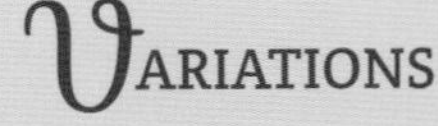

Variations

These little dolls are easy to customize. Get creative with clothing styles and accessories to make your own unique doll!

Horse

There are few animals in human history that have been more revered than the horse. The horses that you make using your pin looms and this pattern can capture a sense of the magic of that animal. As you work with this design, whether you make a horse as a toy for a child or a soft sculpture, I hope that you enjoy the excitement, the thrill to discover what is possible through the small squares of cloth that you have woven.

Finished Measurements

7" x 6" (18 x 15 cm)

Tools

- 2" x 2" pin loom
- 4" x 4" pin loom
- 2" x 4" pin loom
- 4" x 6" pin loom
- Size G-6 (4.0 mm) crochet hook
- Tapestry needle

Yarn

Medium worsted (weight category 4) acrylic yarn

- 37 yd. (34 m) brown
- Scrap amount (less than 1 yd. [0.9 m]) black

Notions

- Polyester fiberfill
- Chenille sticks
- Permanent marker

Instructions

1. Weave in brown yarn:
   - One 4" x 6" weavie
   - One 4" x 4" weavie
   - One 2" x 2" weavie
   - Four 2" x 4" weavies

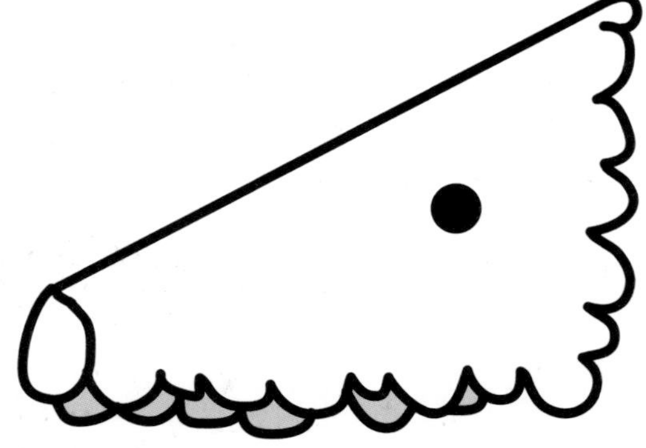

2. Fold down one corner of the 2" x 4" weavie and sew it to the two adjacent sides of the square, as shown in the illustration. Continue the seam under the horse muzzle to form a blunted cone. Stuff the piece a little to help shape the horse head.

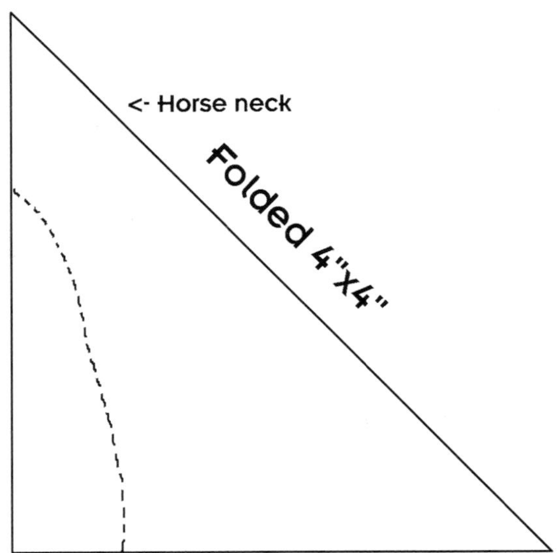

3. Use the 4" x 4" to form horses's neck, following the diagram. Insert the head into neck and sew them together using overcast stitch. Stuff the head and neck.

4. Fold the 4" x 6" weavie in half and join the layers together with single crochet, leaving a 1½" to 2" (4 to 5 cm) opening in the long side for the head. Turn the body right side out and stuff it. Insert the head and neck assembly into the body and sew it in place.
5. Cut four 8" (20 cm) lengths of chenille stick and fold them in half. Roll a doubled chenille stick up in a 2" x 4" weavie and sew along the length of the rolled-up weavie to secure. Repeat with the other three chenille sticks.
6. Place one leg on the outside of the body against one of the corners and stitch it to the body using overcast stitch. Add stitches between the leg and body to stabilize it. Attatch the other three legs, being careful to place them at the same height. If the legs are attached securely and are all about the same length, the horse should be able to stand on its own.
7. Crochet the ears as follows: Chain 4; skip the first chain, half double crochet in the next 2 chains, single crochet in the last chain. Fasten off, leaving a long tail. Make a second ear in the same way. Use the tapestry needle to pull the tail of yarn on each ear back into the head to attach them on either side of the head, then stitch the bases of the ears in place with the same color yarn.
8. Use black yarn to add eyes, a mane, and a tail. You can wrap black yarn around the ends of the legs for hooves. Use a black permanent marker to draw nostrils. Weave in all ends.

Variation: Twig Horse

For the horse with twig legs, I used a bulky (weight category 5) yarn in red tweed; this variation requires only 22 yd. (20 m) of yarn. Omit the four 2" x 4" weavies for the legs. Instead, find four thin, gnarled twigs about 6" to 8" (15 to 20 cm) long (you will trim them shorter after assembly).

Follow the instructions for the horse through step 4. Then use two crochet hooks to pry open the weave at one corner of the horse body and insert a twig. Use matching yarn and tapestry needle to wrap and stitch legs in place: Run the yarn into the horse body close to the twig, and stitch in and out of the body, pulling the yarn tight around the twig to secure it. Then bring the yarn out right by the twig and wrap it around the twig tightly for ¼" to ⅜" (6 to 10 mm). Run the needle back through the yarn wraps to secure the yarn. Repeat this process for the other three legs.

Trim the twigs to the desired length. Keep in mind that they do not have to be perfectly even. They are intended to give the impression of legs and movement rather than exactly reproducing the appearance of a horse's leg.

Sheep

This little primitive-style sheep looks like it stepped out of an illustration from the 1800s. The body is made with two different yarns: Thick curly yarn is wound on the loom for the first three layers, then regular white worsted weight is used for the weaving. This gives the piece a "thick-and-thin" look. It is also much easier to weave using the thinner yarn.

Finished Measurements

3½" x 5" (9 x 12.5 cm)

Tools

- 2" x 2" pin loom
- 4" x 6" pin loom
- Size G-6 (4.0 mm) crochet hook
- tapestry needle

Yarn

- 8 yd. (7 m) bulky (weight category 5) curly white yarn
- 3 yd. (2.7 m) white medium worsted (weight category 4) or lighter yarn
- 4 yd. (3.7 m) of black heather medium worsted (weight category 4) yarn

Notions

- One 12" (30 cm) chenille stick
- Polyester fiberfill
- Rubber cement

Instructions

1. Weave one 4" x 6" weavie, using the thick curly yarn for the first three layers and weaving with the regular white worsted weight yarn. Weave one 2" x 2" weavie in black.

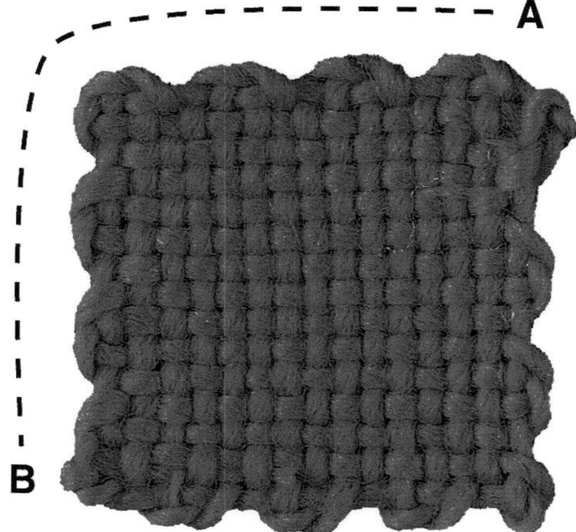

2. Single crochet around two sides of the 2" x 2" weavie, as shown above; corner #3, as indicated on the loom (there is a cluster of three loops in that corner), should be in the center of the two crochet sides. Do not chain 2 at the corner. Fold the two crochet sides together and whipstitch, starting at the corner. This will form a little triangular sheep head.

3. Fold the 4" x 6" weavie in half to form a 3" x 4" (7.5 x 10 cm) piece and single crochet join the three open sides, leaving a 1" (2.5 cm) gap at the top of one of the short sides. Turn the piece inside out and stuff. Insert the head into the hole and stitch in place using the white worsted yarn.

Variation

Make a colorful blanket for the sheep by weaving a 2" x 4" weavie (or sewing two or three 2" x 2" weavies together). Use slip stitch or your choice of stitch styles to decorate your primitive sheep blanket. You'll need about 4 yd. (3.7 m) of yarn in the main color for the blanket plus small amounts of yarn in coordinating colors.

Display Options

This little sheep makes a wonderful addition to a primitive assembly on shelf or table. Add a yarn loop from neck to rump to turn it into a Christmas tree ornament or a very special gift.

4. Make the ears as follows: Using the black yarn, chain 6. Skip the first chain and single crochet in the remaining 5 chains; fasten off, leaving a long tail. Repeat to make a second ear. Use a tapestry needle to pull the tail of yarn attached to each ear back into the head to attach an ear on each side. Stitch the base of each ear in place with black yarn to secure.
5. Cut the chenille stick into two 6" (15 cm) lengths. Using one or two crochet hooks, open a hole on either side of the sheep at the back corner and run one of the chenille sticks through the material and back out, so that there are two 3" (7.5 cm) lengths of chenille sticking out. Fold the chenille stick up on each side to make two doubled legs about 1½" (4 cm) long. Dab some rubber cemet on the chenille stick and let it dry (this gives a good foundation to help secure the yarn wraps). Wrap each leg with the dark heather yarn, starting at the bottom and running the dark yarn into the body at the top. Repeat at the front lower corner for the front legs. Weave in all ends.

Dog

This dog was the first of my small animal patterns and people have really taken to it. This pattern produces a sturdy, confident little dog who can send a message about your love and care for others. It does not call for enormous amounts of yarn and I think you will be surprised at how quickly you can make one. So if you have people in your life who need to know they are supported and loved, give them a dog.

Finished Measurements

4" x 4½" (10 x 11.5 cm)

Tools

- 2" x 2" pin loom
- 4" x 4" pin loom
- Size G-6 (4.0 mm) crochet hook
- Tapestry needle

Yarn

Medium worsted (weight category 4) rough-spun wool yarn

- 20 yd. (18 m) main color
- Scrap amount (less than 1 yd. [0.9 m]) contrasting color for ears, nose, and eyes

Notions

- Two chenille sticks
- Polyester fiberfill

Small projects like this one are great places to use variegated or handspun yarn since only a small amount is needed.

Instructions

1. Weave six 2" x 2" weavies and one 4" x 4" weavie in the main color.

2. Making the head: Bring two adjacent sides of a 2" x 2" weavie together to form a cone; fold in the tip of the cone for a blunter shape, then whipstitch the sides together. Add a little stuffing to get a better sense of its shape. You may want to push the muzzle in more to represent a boxer-like breed or make it very pointy for more of a Doberman look.
3. Making the neck: Fold a second 2" x 2" weavie diagonally and slide one end of it into the head. Sew these two pieces together, then stuff the head and neck.

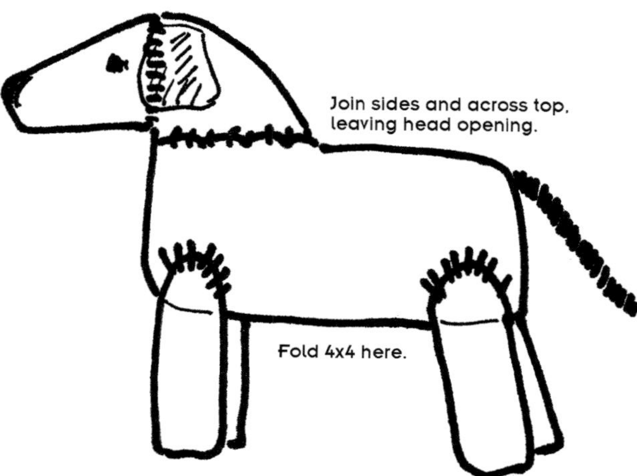

4. Making the body: Fold a 4" x 4" weavie in half. Join the edges together using single crochet, leaving a 2" (5 cm) opening on one end of the longer side for the head and neck. Turn the piece inside out and stuff it. Insert the neck into the hole you left for it and sew it in place.
5. Cut four 2" (5 cm) lengths of chenille stick. Roll each of the remaining 2" x 2" weavies around a chenille stick and sew along the length of each rolled-up weavie, so that you have four rolled up, slightly stiff legs. Flatten the top of each leg and sew it to the outside of the body; stitch between the leg and body as well for extra stability.

TIP: You may notice that I did not suggest closing the ends of the legs. I find that when the ends are left open they look like paws and add stability. However, you may prefer to add a few stitches to the ends of the legs to close them.

6. Add nose and eyes in fine black yarn or crochet thread.
7. Make the ears: With the main color or a contrasting color, chain 6; double crochet in the second chain from the hook and in the next 3 chains, single crochet in last chain. Repeat to make a second ear.
8. Attach the ears to the head, using yarn that matches the ear color. These ears have a tendency to stick out and can make the dog look a little goofy. If you want a more dignified-looking dog, tack the ears down or flip them over before sewing them on. Weave in all ends.
9. Loop a 4" (10 cm) length of chenille stick through the stitching near the dog's spine, and bring the two halves of the chenille stick together to create a 2" (5 cm) tail. Wrap the tail with yarn and run the yarn into the body to secure it. You may want to add a drop of glue at the tip of the tail to help secure the yarn.

VARIATION

Of course, dogs come with enormous variation of ear shape and tail length. If you prefer pointy ears on a dog, see the directions for the pig or cat ears.

Cat

Cats come in lots of colors. My favorites are the ones with orange tiger stripes, which I tried to reproduce here. This design is easy enough that you might find yourself making an entire cat family.

Finished Measurements

3" x 1½" (7.5 x 4 cm) (not counting tail)

Tools

- 2" x 2" pin loom
- 2" x 4" pin loom
- Size G-6 (4.0 mm) crochet hook
- Tapestry needle

Yarn

Medium worsted (weight category 4) yarn

- 3¼ yd. (3 m) tan
- 3¼ yd. (3 m) orange

Notions

- Chenille stick
- Scrap amount (less than 1 yd. [0.9 m]) black crochet thread

If you want to make a solid-colored cat, you will need 6½ yd. (6 m) total of whatever yarn you pick.

Instructions

1. Weave one 2" x 4" weavie and one 2" x 2" weavie, winding the first two layers of yarn in tan, then winding the last layer and weaving with orange.

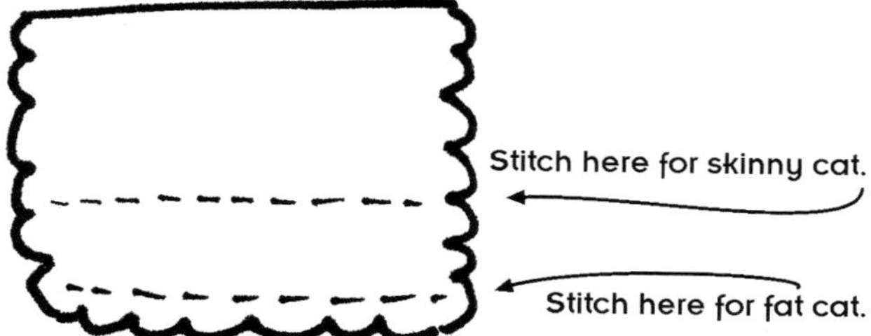

2. Fold the 2" x 4" weavie in half and single crochet around the open edges, leaving a 1" (2.5 cm) opening for the head at one corner. If you want a rather fat cat, go all the way around the width of the fabric. If you want a slimmer cat, slip stitch across the weavie a little way from the bottom edge, leaving some fabric that you will turn to the inside of the body. Turn the body inside out and and stuff.

3. Stitch a loose circle on the 2" x 2" weavie and pull the ends of the stitching to gather the edges, making a pocket in the middle. Add stuffing to the middle to create a marble-sized head. Take some stitches through the gathered ends to produce a smoother neck. Place the head and neck into the body opening and stitch in place.
4. Crochet two ears as follows: Chain 3, skip first chain, single crochet in next chain; fasten off. Sew the ears to either side of the head.
5. Braid a 2" (5 cm) tail using same colors the body is made from. Use a tapestry needle to pull the tail into the body and take a few tiny stitches to secure.
6. Cut two 5" (13 cm) pieces of chenille stick. Double over to produce two 2½" (6 cm) pieces. Run one piece through the front of the body and bend to form the front legs; do the same in the back of the body. Wrap the legs with yarn and run the yarn into the body to secure. You can add a dab of rubber cement or other glue to the bottom of the leg to better secure the yarn.
7. Stitch the eyes and nose with black crochet thread. Weave in all ends.

Mama and Baby Pig

This farm set began with a dog, a sheep, and a horse. But you can't have an old-fashioned farm without pigs and piglets. Mama pig is not complete without a herd of babies. And the babies aren't complete without little tags of Velcro stitched to their noses so that they can cuddle up to their mama and nurse.

Finished Measurements

Mama Pig: 6" x 4" (15 x 10 cm)
Baby Pig: 2" x 1½" (5 x 4 cm)

Tools

- 2" x 2" hand loom
- 4" x 4" hand loom
- 4" x 6" hand loom
- Size G-6 (4.0 mm) crochet hook
- Tapestry needle

Yarn

Pink medium worsted (weight category 4) acrylic yarn

- For Mama Pig: 35 yd. (32 m)
- For Baby Pig: 3 yd. (2.7 m)

Notions

- Polyester fiberfill
- 2 chenille sticks
- Rubber cement
- Black crochet thread
- Round piece of Velcro, ¼" (6 mm) in diameter

Instructions

Mama Pig

1. Weave:
   - One 4" x 6" weavie
   - One 4" x 4" weavie
   - Four 2" x 2" weavies
2. Fold the 4" x 6" weavie in half to get a 4" x 3" weavie. Starting at the folded edge, slip stitch in a curve around the back to make a rounded rump; when you get to the edge, single crochet down the side and across the bottom edge, leaving the other side (the neck) open.
3. Turn the body inside out and stuff.
4. Bring two adjacent sides of a 4" x 4" weavie together to form a cone; fold in ⅓" (8 mm) of the tip of the cone for a blunter shape, then single crochet the sides together. This will be the head. Turn the piece inside out and stuff it. Slide the back of the cone into the body until only the head part is showing and sew in place.
5. Cut four 4" pieces of chenille stick and bend them in two. Roll each doubled chenille stick up in a 2" x 2" square and sew along the length of the rolled-up weavie to secure. Sew the ends of the rolls closed. These are the legs.
6. Place one end of a leg very close to the bottom of one corner of the pig body and sew all the way around the leg to secure. Attach the other three legs in the same manner.
7. Crochet an ear as follows: Chain 6, skip 1 chain, single crochet in next chain, half double crochet in next chain, double crochet in next 2 chains, fasten off. Repeat to make a second ear. Pull the yarn attached to the ear into the head and back through the body to attach the ear to the head, then sew the ear in place. Repeat with the other ear.
8. Work satin stitch with pink yarn around the nose to better define its shape.
9. Add eyes using black crochet thread. Weave in all ends.
10. Wind a short piece of pink chenille stem around a skewer to give it a spiral shape, then insert the chenile stem into the rump for a short, curly tail.

Baby Pig

1. Weave one 2" x 2" weavie.
2. Fold the weavie in half and sew along the bottom edge with overcast stitch to form a tube.
3. Using a pen or finger to maintain tube shape, run the yarn across one end of the tube, crisscrossing from several directions, to sew the end closed.
4. Stuff the tube three-quarters of the way full with fiberfil.
5. Pinch the open end closed and wrap it tightly with several turns of yarn to make a tiny snout. Run a few stitches through the wrapping to secure it.
6. Crochet an ear as follows: Chain 3, single crochet in second chain from hook, half double crochet in last chain, fasten off. Repeat to make a second ear. Pull the yarn attached to the ear into the head and back through the body to attach the ear to the head, then sew the ear in place. Repeat for the other ear.
7. Cut two 1½" (4 cm) pieces of chenille stick. Run one chenille stick through the front of the pig's body and bend to represent the two front legs. Dab with a little rubber cement and let dry to give a better foundation for the yarn wraps. Wrap the legs with pink yarn, running the end of the yarn back into the body to secure. Repeat with the back legs.
8. Add eyes using black crochet thread. Weave in all ends.
9. Sew or glue the ¼" (6 mm) dot of hook-side Velcro to the baby pig's nose.

Chicken

This tiny chicken makes a wonderful accompaniment for the Amish dolls. These were made with a fluffy bouclé yarn, which gives a nice feathery look, woven with a sport-weight yarn. The smooth yarn is much easier to weave with, and it does not diminish the feathery look. You could substitute any type of feathery or fluffy yarn for the bouclé.

Finished Measurements

1½" x 2½" (3.8 x 6.3 cm)

Tools

- 2" x 2" pin loom
- Tapestry needle

Yarn

- 4 ft. (1.2 m) soft white bulky (weight category 5) bouclé yarn
- 2 ft. (0.6 m) white fine (weight category 2) yarn
- Scrap amount (less than 1 yd. [0.9 m]) of red medium worsted (weight category 4) yarn
- Scrap amount (less than 1 yd. [0.9 m]) of yellow medium worsted (weight category 4) yarn

Notions

- Polyester fiberfill
- Plastic beads (optional)

Instructions

1. Weave one 2" x 2" square, winding the first three layers with the bouclé yarn, and weaving with the smooth yarn.

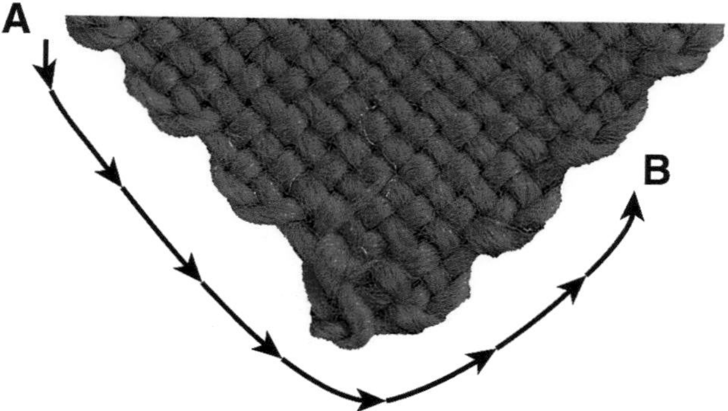

2. Fold the weavie on the diagonal and sew the two open sides together with overcast stitch, leaving an opening at one end.
3. Turn the piece inside out and stuff, adding plastic beads to the tummy area to help keep the chicken upright.
4. Sew the open end (the tail) closed with overcast stitch. Weave in all ends.
5. Add three or four loops of red yarn to the head for a comb.
6. Add one loop of yellow yarn to the front of the head for a beak.

Cow

The cow was requested by a number of family members, who, after seeing the woven people, chicken, sheep, horse, pig, dog, and cat, asked, "Where's the cow?" Here's the cow.

Finished Measurements

4½" x 7" (11 x 18 cm)

Tools

- 2" x 2" pin loom
- 2" x 4" pin loom
- 4" x 6" pin loom
- Size G-6 (4.0 mm) crochet hook
- Tapestry needle

Yarn

Medium worsted (weight category 4) yarn
- 40 yd. (37 m) light brown
- Scrap amount (less than 1 yd. [0.9 m]) dark brown

Notions

- Chenille sticks
- Permanent marker

Instructions

1. Weave:
   - Two 4" x 6" weavies in light brown
   - Two 2" x 4" weavies in light brown
   - Four 2" x 2" weavies in light brown
2. Place the 4" x 6" weavies one on top of the other and single crochet around the edges, rounding the corners as you join by cutting across each corner with a slip stitch. Leave a 2" (5 cm) opening at the top of one narrow side for the head.
3. Form a loose cone from one of the 2" x 4" weavies. Sew the tip of the cone closed with overcast stitch.
4. Fold the second 2" x 4" weavie in half, single crochet along the edge to make a 2" (5 cm) wide tube, and turn it inside out. This will be the cow's neck. Slip the back of the head into the tube and sew it in place. Stuff the neck and head.
5. Insert end of the neck into the body opening and sew it in place. (It may feel as though you have just wasted a lot of time making the 2" x 4" neck piece, since almost all of it will be inserted into the body, but it is needed.)
6. Crochet the cow ear as follows: Chain 6, half double crochet in second chain from hook, double crochet in next chain, half double crochet in next stitch, single crochet in next stitch, fasten off. Repeat for other ear. Attach the ears near the top of the head.
7. For horns, take a 6" (15 cm) length of chenille stem and fold in half. Shape the 3" (7.5 cm) doubled piece into a crescent and wrap it with light brown yarn. Whipstitch the horns to the cow's forehead.
8. For the tail, make a braid 3" long from two strands of dark brown yarn and one light brown. Knot the bottom of the braid and trim the yarn a little below the knot to leave a short fringe. Attach the braid to the cow's rump.
9. Cut four doubled lengths of chenille stick 4" (10 cm) long, and fold each piece in half. Roll each doubled chenille stem up in a 2" x 2" square and sew along the length of the rolled-up weavie to secure.
10. Place one of the legs at one of the corners corners of the body and sew it to the body with overcast stitch. Add some stitches between the leg and the body to further stabilize it. Repeat with the other three legs, being careful to make them even lengths so that the cow can stand on its own.
11. Add eyes to the cow with dark brown yarn. Use a permanent marker to add nostrils. Weave in all ends.

Barn and House Totes

You can make your own purse handle using 12" (30 cm) of 5⁄16" (8 mm) (outside measure) vinyl tubing and two ¾" (2 cm) D rings. Drop a tapestry needle attached to a piece of thin yarn through the vinyl tubing to thread the yarn through. Tie the end of the thin yarn to several strands of red yarn (as many as will fit through the tube) and use the thin yarn to pull them through the tubing. Tie these strands of red yarn to a the D rings on either end of the tube. Use the roof color of yarn to attach the newly constructed purse handle to each end of the peak of the barn roof.

The house and the barn complete the farm set. They give the animals and people somewhere to live (as well as fulfilling the practical need for somewhere to store the little toys). Simple toys like this give children an opportunity to create their own imaginative games. The house or barn adds to the possibilities for creative play.

Finished Measurements

6" x 6" x 4" (15 x 15 x 10 cm)

Tools

- 4" x 4" pin loom
- 4" x 6" pin loom
- Size G-6 (4.0 mm) crochet hook
- Tapestry needle
- Sewing needle

Yarn

Medium worsted (weight category 4) wool, acrylic, or wool-acrylic blend yarn

Barn

The barn is red with white trim, a gray roof, a brown bottom and a brown interior.

- 55 yd. (50 m) red
- 25 yd. (23 m) white
- 85 yd. (78 m) brown
- 30 yd. (27 m) gray heather

House

The house is white with black trim, a dark gray roof, a brown bottom, and a maroon interior.

- 80 yd. (73 m) white
- 15 yd. (14 m) brown
- 75 yd. (69 m) maroon
- 30 yd. (27 m) charcoal heather
- Small amount of dark gray or black

Notions

For each tote, you will need:

- Two 3" x 3" (8 x 8 cm) and and five 3" x 5" (8 x 13 cm) pieces of cardboard
- Approximately 6 sq. ft. (0.6 m^2) of quilt batting or thick felt
- 6" (15 cm) Velcro strip
- Plastic purse handle
- White sewing thread

Instructions

Barn

1. Weave:
   - Two 4" x 6" weavies in red
   - Four 4" x 4" weavies in red
   - Six 4" x 6" weavies in brown
   - Two 4" x 4" weavies in brown
   - Two 4" x 6" weavies in gray heather
2. For each piece of carboard, cut two pieces of batting in the same size. Sandwich each piece of cardboard between the two pieces of batting.
3. Match up a red 4" x 6" weavie and a brown 4" x 6" weavie. Single crochet with white yarn around the edge to join them, with the red weavie facing you. Stop about halway around to tuck a 3" x 5" cardboard and batting sandwich inside, then finish the join. Repeat with another pair of 4" x 6" weavies. Do the same with two sets of red and brown 4" x 4" weavies. These pieces are the walls of the barn.
4. Join two brown 4" x 6" weavies together in the same way for the bottom of the barn.
5. Use gray yarn to join the 4" x 6" gray heather weavies with the two remaining 4" x 6" brown weavies as in step 3, for the two halves of the roof.
6. Fold a red 4" x 4" weavie in half diagonally, insert a piece of batting cut in a triangle shape, and single crochet around the open sides in white. Repeat to make a second roof gable.
7. Add decorative stitching to the walls and to the triangle gable pieces for windows and doors, as shown in the diagram.

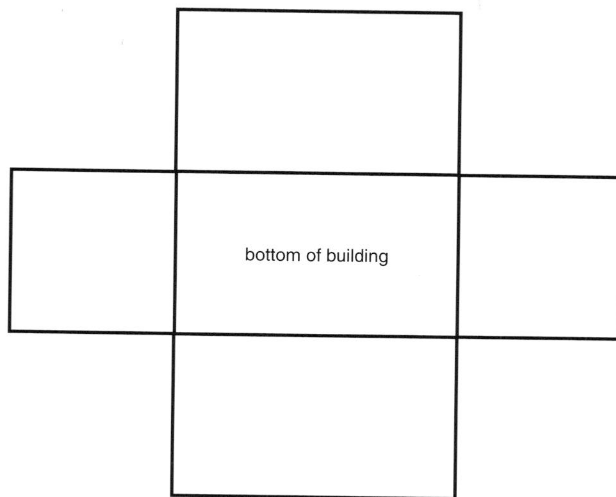

8. Whipstitch the four walls to the bottom with white yarn. Fold the walls up to form a box with the red sides on the outside and whipstitch the sides together.
9. Work a row of half double crochet along the top edge of each 4" x 6" wall with white yarn. These tabs will assist in attaching the roof.
10. Use the sewing needle and white thread to sew the loop side of the Velcro strip to the half double crochet tab on the front side of the house.
11. Whipstitch the two roof pieces together with gray yarn, then whipstitch the two gable pieces to the ends of the roof (still with gray), with the brown sides of the roof pieces to the inside.
12. Using the gray yarn, attach the purse handle to each end of the peak of the roof.
13. Place the roof evenly on the top of the house; it should extend about ¾" over both sides. With brown yarn, whipstitch the white tab without the Velcro to the underside of the roof, approximately ¾" (2 cm) from the edge of the roof.
14. Stitch the hook side of the Velcro strip to the underside of the roof directly above the loop side strip on the front wall. Weave in all ends.

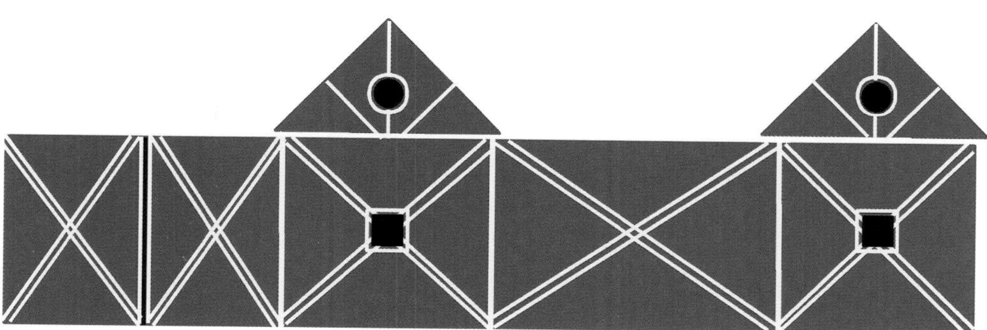

House

1. Weave:
   - Two 4" x 6" weavies in white
   - Four 4" x 4" weavies in white
   - One 4" x 6" weavie in brown
   - Five 4" x 6" weavies in maroon
   - Two 4" x 4" weavies in maroon
   - Two 4" x 6" weavies in charcoal heather
2. For each piece of carboard, cut two pieces of batting in the same size. Sandwich each piece of cardboard between the two pieces of batting.
3. Match up a white 4" x 6" weavie and a maroon 4" x 6" weavie. Single crochet with white yarn around the edge to join them, with the white weavie facing you. Stop about halway around to tuck a 3" x 5" cardboard and batting sandwich inside, then finish the join. Repeat with another pair of 4" x 6" weavies. Do the same with two sets of maroon and white 4" x 4" weavies. These pieces are the walls of the house.
4. Join the weavies for the bottom of the house—the brown 4" x 6" weavie and a maroon 4" x 6" weavie—in the same way.
5. Use charcoal heather yarn to join the 4" x 6" charcoal heather weavies with the two remaining 4" x 6" maroon weavies as in step 3, for the two halves of the roof.
6. Fold a white 4" x 4" weavie in half diagonally, insert a piece of batting cut in a triangle shape, and single crochet around the open sides in white. Repeat to make a second roof gable.
7. Embroider the windows and doors on the walls and the triangle gable pieces, as shown in the diagram.
8. Whipstitch the four white walls to the bottom with white yarn. Fold the walls up to form a box with the white sides on the outside and whipstitch the sides together.
9. Work a row of half double crochet along the top edge of each 4" x 6" wall with white yarn. These tabs will assist in attaching the roof.
10. Use the sewing needle and white thread to sew the loop side of the Velcro strip to the half double crochet tab on the front side of the house.
11. Whipstitch the two roof pieces together with charcoal yarn, then whipstitch the two gable pieces to the ends of the roof (still with charcoal), with the maroon sides of the roof pieces to the inside.
12. Using the charcoal yarn, attach the purse handle to each end of the peak of the roof.
13. Place the roof evenly on the top of the house; it should extend about ¾" over both sides. With maroon yarn, whipstitch the white tab without the Velcro to the underside of the roof, approximately ¾" (2 cm) from the edge of the roof.
14. Stitch the hook side of the Velcro strip to the underside of the roof directly above the loop side strip on the front wall. Weave in all ends.

Variation

In addition to filling the need for a good barn for the pin loom animals, either house or barn would make a fun purse for a little girl. If you decide to make one with more interest in its purse-like qualities, consider adding more decoration to the outside, like tiny flower-covered vines or buttons in the shape of cats or dogs.

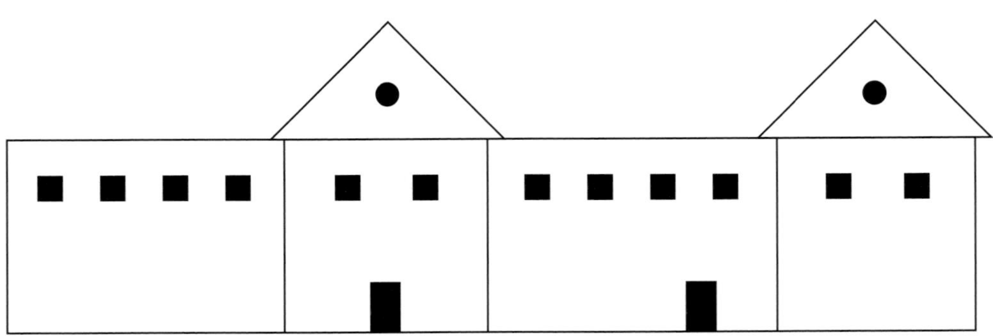

Acknowledgments

Pin loom projects begin with a lot of weaving. These projects came about only with the help of a number of very kind and supportive people, who also proved themselves to be great fiber artists. I want to thank the following people: Carolyn and Abigail Vance, who stood up at the beginning of these projects and gave me hope; Kerry Paarmann, for supporting me with weaving, conversation, and bike riding; Ambry Brave Heart, a very young weaver who politely objected when I said that she was probably too young and then demonstrated just how capable she was; Brenda Peterson, for months of support and hard work; and especially Teresa Rohlk, for her unstinting support—many of the most challenging projects would not have come about without for her work and assistance. Finally, I want to thank my husband, Jerry, for always being there and for continually supporting me with hands and heart.

Resources

Eloomanation.com

Want more information on all things pin loom? Check Eloomanation first. This site gives the history of the variety of hand looms and pin looms that have been made throughout the years, with innumerable resources. You can find detailed instructions for winding and weaving the 4" x 4" loom as well as lots of weaving patterns.

The site has downloadable copies of all the old Weave-It and Loomette pattern and instruction books. You'll find interesting, albeit dated, clothing patterns among these. If you have been searching for a pattern for a bed jacket or a hand-woven bathing suit, the old Weave-It pattern books have it! Eloomanation is also one of several sites where people are sharing their incredible contemporary patterns for pin looms.

Looms

If you're lucky, you can find a beautiful vintage pin loom for sale on eBay or another website. If you're crafty, you can make your own (see instructions on page 4). But the easiest way to get started weaving right away is to buy a pin loom from one of the sources listed below. (With the resurgence of the pin loom, you may soon be able to find some of these looms in major craft stores as well as online.)

Schacht Spindle

www.schachtspindle.com

Schacht Spindle has just released the newest and definitely coolest iteration of the pin loom, the Zoom Loom. Redesigned with the weaver in mind for ease of use and consistent cloth quality, the Zoom Loom comes with clear directions and some clever project ideas. You can see the complete instructions for winding and weaving the Zoom Loom at www.schachtspindle.com/instructions/weaving/zoomloom.pdf. They have also produced a helpful video showing the winding and weaving process. The Zoom Loom is available through Schacht dealers.

Hazel Rose Looms

www.hazelroselooms.com

A leader in producing lovely, lasting looms in a variety of styles that encourage a number of weaving techniques, including bias weaving. The Multi-Loom series is their version of the Weave-It-type pin loom.

U~Weave Looms

www.u-weave-looms.com

This site fills custom orders for pin looms in common and uncommon sizes.

Weaving Needles

As discussed on page 3, you need a long, blunt needle to do the weaving on your pin loom. New looms come with a weaving needle, but if you buy a used one that has lost its needle or if you make your own, you will need to purchase a weaving needle. Below are some manufacturers and sources I've found for suitable needles. Some are brands that may be found at major craft stores; others are online retailers with specialty products.

Dritz

Dritz produces upholstery needles (sold in a 4-pack, which includes a 6" [15 cm], 8" [20 cm], 10" [25 cm], and 12" [30 cm] needle) and Soft Sculpture doll needles, available in various lengths. The tips of these needles must be rounded off before they can be used for weaving.

Bates

Bates makes a 5" (12.5 cm) weaving needle, which is a great size for weaving on 2" x 2" looms and can be used on the 4" x 4" loom as well (although a 6" [15 cm] needle is a better choice for the larger loom). This needle is rounded off, which is essential. However, it is comparatively thick and may not fit through the gaps in some pin looms.

Lacis

www.lacis.com

This online sewing and needlework supplier carries a "Weave-It" weaving needle, 6" (15 cm) long with a blunt point. This appears to be the same needle that comes with the Schacht Zoom Loom.

Upholstery Stuff

www.upholsterystuff.com

The online retailer carries a 6" (15 cm) straight needle; the tip of this needle must be rounded off before it can be used as a weaving needle.